SWAT

LEADERSHIP

AND TACTICAL

PLANNING

This book is dedicated to all SWAT team leaders who have experienced the trials and triumphs of tactical leadership.

SWAT

LEADERSHIP

AND TACTICAL

PLANNING

The SWAT Operator's Guide to Combat Law Enforcement

Tony L. Jones

Paladin Press · Boulder, Colorado

Also by Tony L. Jones:

SWAT Sniper: Deployment and Control

SWAT Leadership and Tactical Planning:
The SWAT Operator's Guide to Combat Law Enforcement
by Tony L. Jones

Copyright © 1996 by Tony L. Jones
ISBN 0-87364-897-8
Printed in the United States of America

Published by Paladin Press, a division of
Paladin Enterprises, Inc., P.O. Box 1307,
Boulder, Colorado 80306, USA.
(303) 443-7250

Direct inquiries and/or orders to the above address.

Visit our Web site at www.paladin-press.com

CONTENTS

PREFACE

The intent of this book is to assist all tactical entities and operators in planning a successful mission. Desirable leadership traits, command structure, position duties, team configuration, weapons choice and placement, team movement and control, the planning process, warning order, Emergency Operations Center (EOC), Tactical Operations Center (TOC), field command post, intelligence sources, mission considerations, operations order, debriefing, and tactical tips are covered.

I have observed many federal, state, city, and county organizations disregard planning or, more frequently, inadequately plan tactical missions. Sometimes urgency and condensed time events were cited as excuses, or more often the belief that planning isn't necessary was obvious. Either excuse demonstrates the lack of training in planning tactical missions.

Tactical planning is a life insurance policy of sorts. Medical support will be planned and staged for expedience in the event that a SWAT operator, hostage, or suspect requires immediate attention. Identification of mixed departments will be delineated to avoid friendly fire situations. Planned routes of approach and assault will be identified to avoid friendly fire and cross fire situations. Personal reaction time will be heightened by *knowing* what to do instead of *guessing* what to do. Planning readily identifies mission scope and chances of success as weighed by team strength and capabilities.

Tactical planning is a useful investigative tool when reconstructing the scene is required. A well-planned mission will avoid the criminal, civil, and social difficulties a poorly planned mission breeds. Tactical planning can be used to develop solutions to similar situations in the future.

Statements may be made citing the age-old theme, "We have never used formal planning before, so why start now?" A good analogy of this is, "If you have never used your weapon, why carry it?" In tactical planning, small unit leadership traits must be utilized in order to cultivate an effective plan, and subordinate participation is critical. Tactical planning is a *team effort* that ensures understanding, promotes confidence in mission accomplishment, and fosters professionalism.

It is critical to plan from the beginning to the end for all tactical situations. Even if a tactical solution isn't required, practice and real-world training will be realized. File all plans for possible future reference should a similar tactical situation come up. Plan thoroughly and execute the plan with required surprise, speed, and violence of action. If one or more of the elements of surprise, speed, or violence of action is compromised, consider aborting the mission. SWAT member survival and mission success depend on it.

Chapter 1
LEADERSHIP TRAITS

Napoleon's view of leadership was clear: "There are no poor units, only poor commanders." I know this sounds harsh, but the concept is inescapably true. Remember this above all else: "A leader can delegate his authority, but he can *never* delegate his responsibility." The chain of command from the EOC commander to the team leader will be held responsible for all of their subordinates' actions and mission outcome.

A leader who dodges responsibility and blames others for mission failure chooses the coward's route. Team members will note these actions, never forget them, and never trust this leader again! Everyone knows that the leader is human and not infallible. The leader must accept this and remember it. He will gain the respect and loyalty of team members by accepting responsibility for actions performed under his or her span of control.

SWAT leaders will discover a wealth of guidance on leadership traits by researching the various military branches. However, don't forget that the leader is responsible for leading a small paramilitary team, so he must place a civilian twist on a military concept. To obtain an effective balance, the leader must be flexible in technique and personal in application.

FLEXIBLE IN TECHNIQUE

Flexibility is a mission success ingredient due to the wide variety of possible SWAT missions, such as vehicle assault, open-air assault, building assault, and so on. A combination of missions is often likely as well. As the scope of a mission expands, so does the need for flexibility. The flexibility concept may be illustrated in just a simple vehicle assault. If a leader only visualizes and plans for one solution, trouble can arise, leading to the injury or death of all parties involved.

For example, what types of problems must a team leader be prepared to respond to? First, the team leader must *what if* as thoroughly as possible. What if the vehicle is not parked in the optimum position? What if the vehicle is not prepared properly or the team is running behind on their time hack? What if the team is short a member or the distraction device fails? What if not everyone involved departs the stronghold or the adversary does something unexpected? A good team leader will brainstorm the mission with his team in an effort to cover as many possibilities as possible. Flexibility equals preparedness; narrow-minded, one-dimensional thinking can easily result in failure and disaster. Flexibility will often prevent a bad situation from turning into a worse situation.

Manpower constraints will often require flexibility from the team leader. Manpower requirements are formulated by mission type, adversary/hostage numbers, and affected area. A minimum formula is two SWAT operators for every suspect. Next, mission type is considered. Using a vehicle assault plan, for example, a team leader will usually plan to use, at a minimum, six men. However, if six men aren't available, team members will have to pull double duty. Even if the team leader has six men available, he must be flexible in utilizing manpower to cover unexpected circumstances.

Logistics require great flexibility. A leader must use what equipment is available, then adapt it to the mission. Often, as many features and capabilities as possible must be squeezed from a weapon system or tool. For example, a distraction device may be deployed as a diversion, entry tool, and tactical signaling device all at once.

Laws and department rules and regulations may prevent a team leader from choosing a tactic or tool, so once again, flexibility comes into play, such as departmental regulations stating no distraction devices will be used inside a residence if children younger than eight years old are present. The team leader may then decide to deploy the distraction device outdoors as a diversion instead of indoors for entry purposes.

A final example of team leader flexibility may be due to society's views. A society may view automatic weapons as being too militaristic, threatening, or overpowering for law enforcement agencies. In this case the leader may choose the AR-15 rifle series rather than the M16 series.

Flexibility may indeed mean the difference between life or death for the SWAT team and even mission success or failure. It is required in order to adapt to situational constraints, i.e., type of mission, manpower, logistics, departmental rules and regulations, laws, societal views, and so on.

PERSONAL IN APPLICATION

Personal in application refers to what I call a person's "go button." Find out what motivates a person, then cultivate this trait in order to accomplish the mission. Motivation is internal, and for the best long-term performance, one must strive to provide the operator with the object or concept he desires. Examples of personal motivators are belonging to a special team, excelling at a skill recognized by the team, being trusted by the team, being needed by the team, etc. To further clarify, the subordinate may want to be a designated shooter, sniper, scout, mirror man, stealth specialist, crisis specialist, negotiator, rear security, cover man, tactical planner, specialist with a certain weapon, chemical weapons man, or breacher.

It's the SWAT leader's job to find out where the operator belongs versus the operator's desire. If the two coincide, fine; if not, explain and foster other talents. For example, the operator may want to be the rear security for the recognition of being the second most tactically adept person on the team or for the trust the team places on this person. If for some reason you don't want this individual as rear security, you must tell him why, focusing on strengths you see in him. He may see himself as not being tactically proficient enough to be a scout, when the team leader wants him to be the scout. A simple solution here may be to explain that if the team reverses its direction, he will be the scout through necessity, so instead of being a part-time scout, you, as team leader, and the team need him as a full-time scout. Focus on the fact that his maturity, decision-making abilities, sound judgment, and decisiveness are valued. Express the belief that he is the most tactically proficient member of the team. Don't lie; team duties reflect survival chances and mission accomplishment.

Don't follow the common solution of placing an operator in a position so the leader can "keep an eye on him" or "keep him out of the way." If an operator is substandard, replace him, or team efficiency and confidence will suffer. The coddling of a substandard operator is dangerous for everyone and everything involved, from team member survival to mission success.

Can a person be motivated by external means such as ordering compliance? Perhaps, but this is open to debate in reference to the true meaning of motivation. Remember the civilian environment, the short-term results of this act, limitations on performance, and hard feelings. Ordering is best left in the military arena or used in exigent circumstances only. Much more can be gained from an operator who wants to perform compared to one who is forced to perform.

A pitfall to avoid at all costs is the "hotdogger," a person only motivated by self-recognition or self-fulfillment. If a team leader can't control this operator, then he should get rid of him! Sooner or later this person will get another team member hurt or killed. Every team member has an assigned duty, usually integral with another's duty, to facilitate operator safety and mission accomplishment. If the leader has a *me* person instead of a *we* person, he will have a weak team. No matter how "high speed—low drag" the hotdogger is, choose the solid team members who perform as a team.

DECISIVENESS

The SWAT leader must be decisive. Get all the facts, weigh one against the other, then calmly and quickly arrive at a sound decision. Seek ideas from the team members; many sound ideas originate here. The leader will discover that different people view the same circumstances in different ways. Consider as many angles as possible when planning a mission. The leader is not omnipotent; he should therefore *require* team member participation in planning operations. Team members will commit themselves to a greater extent when the plan is viewed as a team plan instead of a domineering plan.

Don't become bogged down and indecisive due to a variety of ideas. Assimilate applicable ideas into the primary and secondary plans. Brief the team on the decided action in a clear, forceful manner. This will lend additional confidence in the plan. When the team members believe in and understand a mission, they will do their best to accomplish it.

INITIATIVE

The real world demonstrates that plans more often than not will deviate to some extent. Here is where the leader will have to display initiative to meet new and unexpected situations with prompt action. If a leader cannot seize the initiative when required, the team members and mission will be at risk. In military slang, "Do what you have to do."

The leader seizes initiative through sound judgment. Sound judgment is the ability to logically weigh the facts as they unfold and then develop possible solutions. Technical knowledge and common sense are the critical factors of sound judgment. Common sense is a personal trait, but technical knowledge is learned. This is why leaders must constantly attend schools and training classes. The leader must train with the team and not set himself up as sole evaluator and keeper of knowledge.

QUALIFICATION

Rank and position alone will not automatically gain the respect and confidence of team members. The team leader must demonstrate to his men that he is qualified both technically and tactically to lead them. The best way to accomplish this is by training with them. The highest praise a leader will hear is when a team member says, "I would follow that man down a cannon barrel." To obtain this level, the leader must, in conjunction with the aforementioned traits, set the example. Share danger and hardship with the team members. Demonstrate a willingness to assume and share these difficulties. The subordinates are not beasts of burden or pieces of equipment. Finally, know the men and look out for their welfare.

Getting to know the men is a big part of team effectiveness. The leader, through careful observation, should note each team member's most and least effective duty positions, leadership potential, preferred weapon, weapons proficiency, and so on. Remember, the most preferred weapon may not be the team member's most proficient weapon. The team leader must participate in as many training sessions, drills, and missions as possible. When the leader automatically knows what each member will do in a variety of situations, the team will be moving as one man, the ultimate team goal.

Looking out for the team's welfare entails the leader taking responsibility for the team's actions and backing the team, as well as attempting to procure the best equipment available. Sharing hardships such as weather, difficult missions, and training helps prevent the unnecessary misuse of personnel. SWAT teams will be much more effective when they view the leader as one of them, and looking out for the men's welfare is the key to achieving this.

Chapter 2

TEAM MECHANICS

As in most organizations, a hierarchy must be developed for effective functioning. The key to effective functioning is effective leadership. A typical hierarchy is depicted in Figure 1 (page 12).

SWAT COMMANDER DUTIES

1. Liaison between SWAT teams and upper management

2. EOC liaison

3. Equipment procurement/logistics

4. Budgeting

5. Team staffing

6. Training guidance

7. Rules, regulations, standard operating procedures (SOPs)

8. Additional duties as required

If the program fails, it is a direct reflection of the SWAT commander's ability to perform. Beware! Many officers want this title, but in name only.

SNIPER COMMANDER DUTIES

1. Liaison between snipers, team leaders, TOC, and SWAT commander

2. Provides guidance on coordination and planning of sniper operations

3. Sniper training and standards development

4. Procurement of equipment

5. Sniper operations logistics and control

If the sniper program fails, it is a direct reflection of the sniper commander's ability to perform. Beware! Many officers want this title, but few want the awesome responsibilities attached to it.

SNIPER LEADER DUTIES

1. Liaison between snipers, SWAT team leaders, and sniper commander

2. First-line supervisor

3. Coordination and planning of sniper operations

4. Implementation of sniper training

5. Recommendation of equipment

6. Team control and logistics

If the sniper program fails, it is a direct reflection of the sniper leader's ability to perform. Beware! This is a difficult position due to pressure from the top and bottom of the hierarchy. The sniper leader will experience more criticism than recognition.

SWAT TEAM LEADER DUTIES

1. Liaison between team members, TOC, SWAT commander, and other teams

2. First-line supervisor

3. Coordination and planning of mission

4. Team training and standards achievement

5. Equipment recommendation

6. Team control and logistics

If the SWAT program fails, it is a direct reflection of the team leader's ability to perform. Beware! Like the sniper leader, this is a difficult position due to pressure from the top and bottom of the hierarchy. The team leader will experience more criticism than recognition.

SNIPER DUTIES

1. Scouting tactical arena

2. Gathering and reporting tactical intelligence

3. Overwatch

4. Subject neutralization

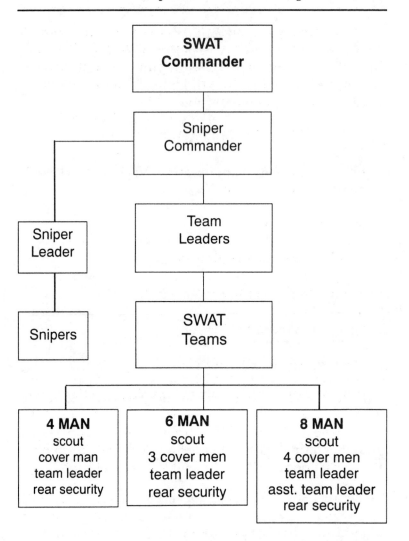

Figure 1: First-line tactical command structure.

If the sniper fails, it is a direct reflection of the program's state of readiness. Individual failure will result in ready and immediate scrutiny by all entities. Snipers are often a central focal point throughout the mission. Carefully evaluate a sniper's failure to make sure his shortcomings are not due to an error on the leader's part. Salvage the man when possible; replace him when necessary.

TEAM MEMBER DUTIES

1. Nuts and bolts of the tactical program

2. Assist team leader in tactical planning

3. Hands-on operations—vehicle assault, building assault, search and clear, hostage rescue, tactical deliveries, etc.

4. "Talk the talk, walk the walk." This means an individual can actually do what he says. Talking is superficial and may be an exaggeration. Walking the walk—doing the deed and performing—is the essence of an operator. Often, the talker is bragging or prevaricating to cover up personal shortcomings. A quiet, sincere individual is often the one who can walk the walk. They are often trustworthy, proficient, and deadly.

If the team member fails, it is a direct reflection of the program's state of readiness. Individual failure will result in ready and immediate scrutiny by the other members. Carefully evaluate a member's failure, and make sure his shortcomings are not due to an error on the leader's part. Salvage the man when possible; replace him when necessary.

TEAM ORGANIZATION

There are generally three types of SWAT team

organizations: the 4-, 6-, and 8-man team. However, these numbers are not static; mission scope specifies team strength.

4-Man Team Organization

The 4-man team consists of a scout, cover man, team leader, and rear security. Be extremely cautious when utilizing 4-man teams, as they have to cover a large area with few personnel.

About the only advantage realized is that the team can be easily controlled by the team leader. The disadvantages are numerous: lack of firepower, lack of weapons variety, lack of security, limited flexibility, and lack of manpower. Remember that the mission assigned must be commensurate with the size of the team. Just one four-way hall intersection, for example, halts this team. (See Figure 2.) The tactical arena can neutralize the team, not to mention the ideal adversary-to-SWAT-member ratio of two to one.

One acceptable use would be to split an 8-man team into two 4-man teams in order to make simultaneous entries into a small area. The consideration here is speed versus security. Be cautious of cross fire possibilities, and reform into the original 8-man team as soon as possible.

6-Man Team Organization

The 6-man team consists of a scout, first cover man, second cover man, team leader, third cover man, and rear security. This team is also easily controlled by the team leader; however, the same disadvantages the 4-man team experiences still exist, but not to the same degree. (See Figure 3.)

Two additional disadvantages exist. The first concerns splitting the team into two 3-man elements, or a 4-man team and a 2-man team; neither is convenient. The second disadvantage occurs with the loss of even one man, which handicaps the team severely. The 4-man

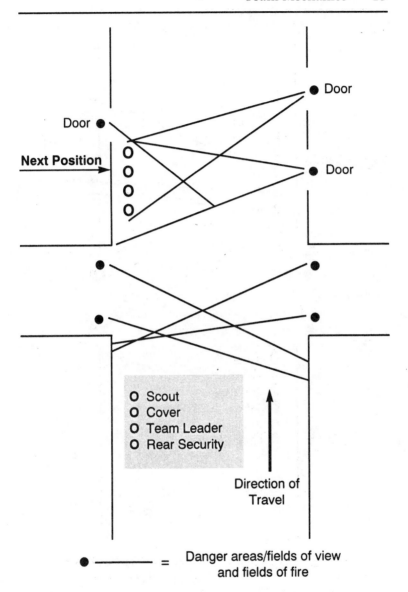

Figure 2: 4-man team organization. Danger areas overwhelm the 4-man team's ability to cover itself. To even cross the intersecting hallway is a dangerous proposition. The danger areas presented by doorways are an additional concern.

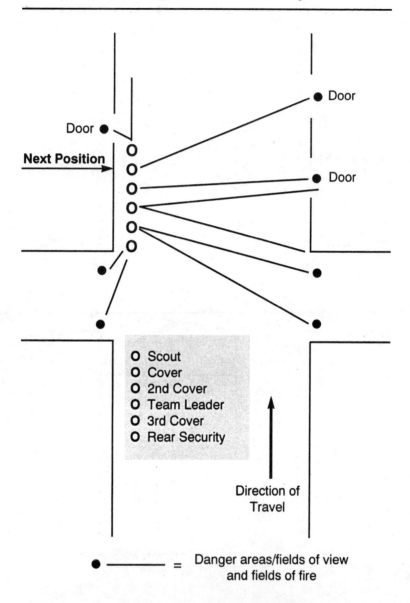

Figure 3: 6-man team organization. The 6-man team is much more capable of covering danger areas. The intersecting hallway can now be crossed safely and the doorways across the hall can be covered as depicted.

team is a minimally staffed team, and two 3-man teams are considered substandard.

Only special circumstances enable two 3-man configurations to be effective. An example would be to simultaneously assault an area from two directions with two 3-man teams or a 4-man/2-man mix. This would only be performed in small areas for short periods of time. The areas covered must be small in order for two 3-man teams to be effective. A special circumstance may develop when there are two entryways into a room, such as an interconnecting type room. A simultaneous assault may be a good way to gain control of such an area with a few men.

Regrouping into the normal group strength is necessary for security reasons and cross fire prevention. In fact, reforming into the original 6-man team is paramount. The 6-man team, in my opinion, is the bare minimum strength for most operations.

8-Man Team Organization

The 8-man team consists of a scout, first cover man, second cover man, team leader, third cover man, fourth cover man, assistant team leader, and rear security. This team provides a great deal of flexibility. The team may operate as two 4-man teams when required, or in various other mixes, such as a 6-man/2-man mix or a 5-man/3-man mix. Reforming into the original 8-man team is required to realize this organization's full potential. This enables two assistant team leaders to aid the team leader in maintaining control at all times. This team is very strong logistically because ample equipment, ammunition, and weapons are at hand. Figure 4 illustrates an 8-man team stack.

TEAM MEMBER RESPONSIBILITIES

The actual labeling of the team members (identifying them by billet) listed in the 4-, 6-, and 8-man teams was

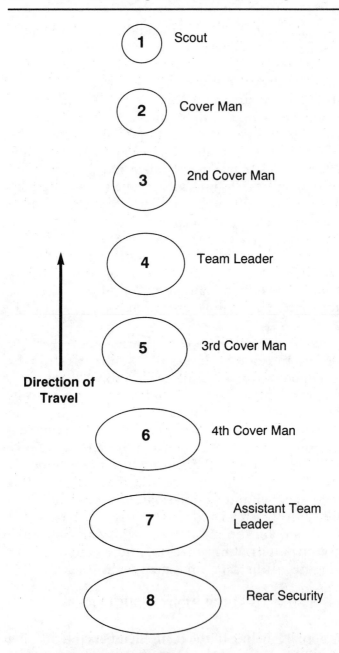

Figure 4: 8-man team stack.

done for expediency. The responsibilities of each position are flexible and tailored to fit the mission. Some general responsibilities for each position are as follows:

TEAM LEADER—Coordinates movements of other members; plans actions and routes to be taken; has overall responsibility for the mission; accounts for his team members.

ASSISTANT TEAM LEADER—Performs the same responsibilities as above when the team splits; takes charge if the team leader is taken out; assists team leader as directed; fills any team position when not utilized in the team leader function.

SCOUT—Leads team from point and reconnoiters his tactical area of responsibility; provides cover at the point position; conducts searches of designated areas; performs other duties as directed by the team leader.

COVER MAN—Provides cover for assigned teammate; covers danger areas as they appear; deploys distraction devices; can be used as an assaulter, hostage handler, arrest team member, evidence control, chemical irritant man, breacher, etc.; is assigned other duties as directed by the team leader.

REAR GUARD—Provides security and protection to the rear of the formation; alternate scout; performs other duties as directed by the team leader.

SNIPER—Two men trained to provide multi-fire support; overwatch for assault teams and containment; provides observation and intelligence. Snipers are the eyes and ears of the TOC. When operating as snipers, they operate under their own chain of command and as a separate entity. When no open-air option is anticipated (sniper mission designed to solve or assist in solving a problem), they are directed to fill an assault team position as required.

TEAM POSITION SELECTION

These team positions are filled by individuals possessing certain attributes, for example:

TEAM LEADER—Selection is based on experience, proven judgment, and capability. Do not choose this person by rank or seniority alone.

ASSISTANT TEAM LEADER—Selection is based on experience, proven judgment, and capability. Once again, do not choose this person by rank or seniority alone.

SCOUT—Most tactically adept person on the team. He is experienced and possesses good judgment and tactical capability. The scout will make numerous decisions without consulting the team leader. When in tense, elongated operations, change this man out with the rear guard so he can come off the razor's edge for awhile, about every 30 minutes or so. Scouts are very aggressive and conscientious. Check on them often because they will push their capabilities to the limit. The best indicator of fatigue is inordinate decision-making measured by their normal responses.

COVER MAN—Selected by size, alertness, and perception. This operator must be able to cover his designated partner. He must be alert at all times and perceive danger areas through skill and experience. He is also chosen for his ability to perform in a variety of positions, such as designated shooter, breacher, grenadier, chemical irritant man, etc.

REAR GUARD—Selected as the second most tactically proficient member of the team. He is also selected for alertness and perception. Alternate this position with the scout when tactically sound to do so. If the formation flips, the rear guard becomes the scout. A common misuse of this position occurs when using it as a dumping ground for weak team members. Don't do this; the importance of this position is obvious.

SNIPERS—Selected by personal attributes such as patience, maturity, loyalty, can-do attitude, reliability, and sound decision-making abilities. He must be tactically adept and be a superb marksman.

Be advised that physical size is sometimes a consideration when choosing an operator for a position. Small personnel are good as scouts because they move around well in tight places and are easier for cover men to shoot around. Don't assign a small person to cover a large person; he won't be able to see. Arrange team personnel by like height when clearing stairs. When covering a mirror man, glance at his hands. If his hands are past the weapon muzzle line of the cover man, the mirror man is uncovered and may get angle shot. Once again, a small team member won't be able to adequately cover a larger team member.

A note on the mirror man. This team member will be using a portable mirror to pan around corners, peer over and under obstacles, and observe tactically dangerous places. The mirror is used as an extension of the head/eye and is much safer than a quick peek. A mirror can be replaced—a head can not. Mirrors are available in many designs.

Cross-training is mandatory due to the ever-changing circumstances in a tactical arena. Every member must be trained in every position. If a team member is taken out, any member may then be tasked to perform the missing member's duties. Specialize, then cross-train.

WEAPONS PLACEMENT

The team leader decides what weapon will be placed in each position as the situation unfolds. This is not suggesting that weapons are passed up or down the formation—rather, team members change out positions as required. The team leader must ensure these changes take place only when it is tactically sound to do so, such as when the team is in a good covered and concealed position. If you can't change out safely, go with what you have. Figure 5 illustrates the necessity for a weapon/personnel change out.

WEAPON CHOICES

HANDGUN—I recommend a high-capacity semiautomatic. Stopping power will be reflected by shot placement. A standard response drill should be employed—two shots to center mass of the body followed by one shot to the head. The head shot is performed because handgun calibers often fail to incapacitate in a rapid manner due to body armor, drug use, will to live, and so on. If the adversary is still mobile after being shot, he may still kill. This is particularly dangerous in close quarters. The head shot prevents this.

The handgun is a good choice for close proximity

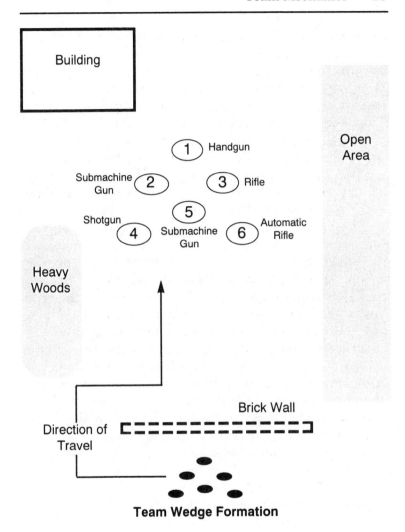

*Figure 5: Weapon/personnel change out. The shotgun is posi-
tioned to cover the woods, submachine gun #2 covers the woods
and building, the handgun covers the building, the rifle covers the
open area, and the automatic rifle covers the open area and can
maneuver as required. Weapons and personnel are positioned prior
to entering the open area. If not, the shotgun and handgun may be
out of their respective effective ranges. The center submachine gun
is in reserve.*

operations such as vehicle assaults, searching and clearing condensed areas, and employing contact shots as required. (A contact shot is performed when grappling with the adversary by pressing the muzzle expeditiously against the adversary and pulling the trigger. This usually motivates him to let go of the SWAT officer.) Night sights are valuable, but remember the operator is still responsible for target identification, so weapon-mounted lights are a plus. The semiautomatic handgun is quick to load by combat or tactical method, and it is also easy to load in the dark.

The handgun is portable, so each member should carry two of the same caliber—one in a drop-leg holster, the other in a tactical vest. I recommend calibers no smaller than 9mm, with .40 caliber and .45 caliber being preferred because the bigger the bullet, the more tissue, organ, and bone damage. Glock's Models 17, 19, 21, 22, and 23 are extremely reliable and simple to operate.

If the handgun fails in close-quarter battle, the operator won't have time to perform immediate action procedures—he must transition to the second handgun or other weapons. Sometimes, the scout only carries handguns to facilitate movement. The caliber should be compatible with the submachine gun for logistics and interchangeability.

The operator press checks this weapon before beginning the operation. To press check the weapon, the operator:

1. Watches his muzzle control

2. Keeps his finger off the trigger

3. Cocks the hammer, if applicable

4. Grasps the slide, moving it to the rear far enough to view a loaded round or to feel a loaded round

5. Returns the slide to battery

6. Returns the hammer to battery

7. Sets the safety as required

Never begin an operation assuming the weapon is hot!

SUBMACHINE GUN—Suppressed models with stable, collapsible stocks are a plus. I recommend H&K's MP5 Series except for the MP5K, which has no stock and is therefore limited in use. A system that fires from the closed bolt is usually the most accurate because the bolt is already forward when the trigger is squeezed, reducing movement. A rate of fire around 850 rounds per minute or slower is best for control purposes. Semiautomatic capability is desirable because it is more accurate and easier to control (10 yards is pushing the full-auto precision-shooting envelope). Check to see if the weapon is fully loaded before starting the operations. To do this:

1. Check the magazine indicator windows, or if a dual-stack magazine is used, observe the position of the top round

2. Insert the magazine

3. Let the bolt go forward

4. Remove the magazine

5. Observe the position of the top round, ensuring that the round is now on the opposite side as before. If yes, the round has been chambered. If no, a bolt over has occurred and the procedure must be repeated.

6. Reinsert the magazine

7. Ensure its seating and the system is ready to rock.

The submachine gun offers firepower, accuracy over the handgun, mid-range coverage, portability, is quick and easy to reload, and is a nice platform for close-quarter combat. If the weapon malfunctions, transition to the handgun to save time in evaluating the stoppage and clearing it. Stopping power will be reflected by shot placement. The standard tactical response should be two two-shot bursts to the body followed by one two-shot burst to the head.

SHOTGUN—The shotgun is unequaled for close-in stopping power and versatility. I suggest the H&K Super 90. Round assortment is vast. Some examples are rifled slug, shock locks, distraction devices, rubber shot, baton rounds, chemical irritant rounds, chemical irritant launching rounds, bird shot, bolo rounds, flechette rounds, and buckshot loads. This weapon platform can be tailored to fit a variety of tactical situations. It is extremely effective for laying down close-proximity suppressive fire. It can be used for mid-range accurate fire, area fire, breaching locks or hinges (frangible slugs made of powdered zinc, dental plaster, etc.), deployment of chemicals, or penetration. The system may be either pump-operated or semiautomatic. Semiautomatics have an edge for one-hand operations and when firing from the prone position. Check the chamber before beginning the operation to ensure the weapon is hot.

SEMIAUTOMATIC/AUTOMATIC RIFLES—Rifles are used for accurate long-range fire, base of fire techniques, and penetration. The M16 series and M177E2 in 5.56 are good. Automatic rifles can be used as a substitute for a general purpose machine gun (GPMG). Only the designated rifleman should fire the rifle on full automatic for fire control purposes. Stopping power is unequaled compared to most small arms. Caliber is determined by size and weight of the rifle and ammunition portability. Checking the weapon's readiness is the same procedure used for the submachine gun.

SNIPER RIFLES—Normally bolt actions capable of minute of angle accuracy or better. Remington's Model 700 PSS in .308 Winchester is tops. It is accurate, powerful, and not affected by environmental conditions at realistic police sniper distances. These are used for precision fire on targets to end the situation, protect overwatch teams, or trim adversary strength. This rifle should be multishot, dependable, and extremely accurate.

GENERAL PURPOSE MACHINE GUN—Must be man-portable, complete with bipod, usually belt fed, with a desirable rate of fire around 550 rounds per minute. The H&K 21 and FN MAG are good choices. This is an extremely specialized weapon used for a base of fire, suppressive fire, and penetration. Be careful: the operator is accountable for every round put down range. Overpenetration is a critical factor as well. This is a good system to deploy from a lightly armored vehicle. Choose a select number of personnel to utilize this system and train them adequately. If just any operator deploys the GPMG, they will more than likely "spray and pray," letting rounds fly high and wide.

PYROTECHNICS

Chemical irritants, smoke, and distraction devices can be valuable tools for mission accomplishment by channeling adversaries into certain areas, causing them to evacuate certain areas, and disrupting their normal functioning. Misuse can heighten tactical difficulties, cause property damage, or even wrongful death.

CHEMICAL IRRITANTS—*Always* follow the manufacturer's specifications in reference to utilization, deployment formulas, storage, and expiration dates. Remember, when the suspect is placed in a chemical environment, SWAT operators may have to fight in that environment. Physical exertion is heightened while wearing a protective mask. The mask is hot, it restricts the operator's vision, and hearing is impaired because he hears himself breathing. Voice communication is impaired, and marksmanship can be affected as well; however, comm systems using bone conduction help solve this problem. Utilize a full face mask with small adjustable canisters. If operators know the suspect has a protective mask, they may avoid chemical usage since no tactical advantage would be realized.

Chemical irritants indoors may linger for long periods of time, cut down on vision, and contaminate other areas. Chemical irritants may cause adversaries or hostages to panic. Leave an exit open, and be ready to handle multiple subjects. A hostage handling team or arrest team is good for this. Never deploy chemical irritants in such a manner as to trap subjects who are holding hostages.

Use irritants sparingly by following usage formulas. Be prepared for the possibility of fire, and only use devices designed for indoor use. The parent department will be responsible for costly decontamination procedures.

Three general choices of chemicals are chloroacetophenone (CN), orthochlorobenzal (CS), and oleoresin capsicum (OC). I prefer OC for ease of cleanup, lessened lethality concerns, and nonflammable delivery choices. (CS is more powerful than CN; CN is a lacremator agent that works on the eye glands, nose and throat, with CS doing the same but also affecting breathing in the chest itself and possibly making the victim nauseous and dizzy.)

All team members should be proficient in their department's chemical delivery systems. These systems include:

1. Blast dispersion

2. Burning

3. Aerosol

4. Projecto jets (man-portable, nonflammable, CO_2-discharged systems about the size of a flamethrower with extended range)

5. Pepper foggers

6. Liquids

7. Weapon-platform projected (shotgun, handgun, or other weapon)

SMOKE—Smoke is used to conceal the team's movement from the suspect's view. A good smoke screen will completely obscure the team's activities but will obscure the subject's position as well. Beware of the suspect who may move to a new location unseen. Smoke is generally used to conceal team movement across open areas. It is also used to conceal movement forward or backward when under fire or "pinned down." Smoke is also used as a signaling device, but it can cause team control problems as a result of wind changes occurring at inopportune times. It can be delivered by hand, weapon, burning, or pepper fogger. Be prepared for fire when using any pyrotechnics.

DISTRACTION DEVICES—Distraction devices are used to facilitate dynamic building entries and vehicle assaults or as signaling devices. Defense Technology of America's Model 25 is a good one. They are designed to distract, disorient, confuse, scare, divert, or slow a suspect's reaction time. Choose a device that:

1. Is nonfragmenting

2. Has a fixed fuse

3. Is not prone to sympathetic detonation (detonating because one near it detonated—a chain reaction)

4. Is bullet resistant

5. Is nonlethal

6. Has a detonation time from 1 to 1 1/2 seconds

Carry them on the leg in a Kevlar-backed carrying system. Consider possible injury to the face, eyes, and chest if sympathetic detonation occurs while using the tactical vest carry technique. Be prepared for smoke and fire. Wear Nomex gloves and hoods for fire protection. An operator shouldn't wear a knit watch cap unless he wants it permanently melted to his head.

SIGHT SYSTEM ENHANCERS

If night vision goggles are considered, choose binocular over monocular. Monocular devices can only be focused on one point at any time, meaning if the operator focuses the device on the weapon sights, he won't be able to see the target, and if he focuses on the target, he won't be able to see the sights. Many devices are dual purpose, being either infrared or ambient light magnifiers. These are fine, but utilize the infrared mode sparingly since it can be picked up by other night vision devices very easily.

Avoid laser sights because operators can make poor use-of-force decisions with them by focusing on the laser beam instead of the adversary's hands. Remember, there is a great difference between target acquisition and target identification. Also remember that lasers work both ways—the adversary can run the beam right back to the operator's position. Lasers are also less efficient in smoke, chemical irritant environments, fog, or foliage. Poor marksmanship habits can also develop due to over-reliance on lasers.

Chapter 3
TEAM MOVEMENT AND CONTROL

The ability of the SWAT team to move as a unit, both when fire is expected and when the team is actually under fire, is essential. Several independently moving operators are vulnerable to a suspect, offer no mutual protection, and may present cross fire situations or casualties from friendly fire. It is the team leader's responsibility to control the team at all times.

Team movement skills are required when SWAT teams are not afforded the opportunity to deploy directly on the target sight. Proper team movement and control enables life-saving immediate action when required.

CONTROL, SECURITY, AND SPEED

The team leader must consider the factors of control, security, and speed whenever the team moves. The factor that is given the greatest weight is generally dictated by the circumstances. For example, control is a major concern in complex assaults, during times of poor visibility due to dense or difficult terrain, or if the team has been split.

Security and speed are a trade-off. The ideal movement would be fast and secure, but usually it is impossible to have both to the same degree desired. The formations to be discussed shortly will illustrate this concept.

Principles of Movement and Control

To ensure that control, security, and speed factors work for the team to the highest degree possible, the team leader must follow four principles of tactical team movement.

1. The first principle is to never move alone. Always move using a minimum of two separate elements mutually supporting each other. For example, one moves, one covers.

2. The second principle is to use covered and concealed routes. Do not move in the open more than is absolutely necessary. This is a danger area likely to attract the suspect's attention and is possibly covered by his weapon. Do not take the most obvious route to the target, such as a driveway to a house (what is known as a high-speed avenue of approach). Even an inept suspect will observe and cover this approach. Use every natural and man-made object that is between the team and the suspect. This conceals the team's approach and protects it from adversary fire.

3. The third principle is to maintain separation. This avoids having two elements so close together that they can be brought under fire from the same suspect's location. The elements may be two SWAT operators or two teams. A general rule of thumb is five meters to the front, rear, left, or right of the next operator. The distance between teams is usually 50 to 100 meters. This distance is measured from the point man to the rear security of the lead team. Figure 6 illustrates maintaining separation. Keep in mind that terrain, poor visibility, and the factors of speed versus security and control may lengthen or shorten these distances.

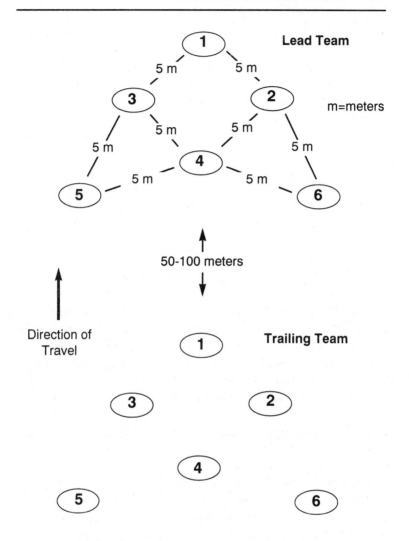

Figure 6: Maintaining separation. #1 scout, #2 cover man, #3 cover man, #4 team leader, #5 cover man, #6 rear security. The lead team is 50 to 100 meters in front of the trailing team. This enables the trailing team to maneuver if the lead team receives fire. Five meters represents the general distance between team members. Team members must also attempt to stagger themselves so that no two members can be hit in one burst of fire. You are not on parade, so a perfectly shaped formation isn't required.

4. The fourth principle is to provide mutually supporting fire. Team members must be prepared to support
each other with weapons fire. The team itself must be
prepared to support the other teams. This principle
masses firepower to either extricate teams or members from a suspect's field of fire or is used to overwhelm the suspect. The longer the operators remain
in a suspect's field of fire, the more casualties will be
sustained. Team members must watch their muzzle
control and never point their weapons at anything
they aren't willing to destroy! The SWAT operator's
finger shouldn't be on the trigger until the weapon's
sights are on an identified target.

BASIC TACTICAL FORMATIONS

During team movement, the team leader has four
basic formations to choose from: wedge, file, line, and
column. Normally, during an operation, the leader will
adapt to the tactical arena by using more than one formation. Each formation is unique in regard to the degree of
control, security, and speed provided. The team leader
must decide which consideration has the greatest weight
related to mission accomplishment. Weapons are placed
in the formation according to their capabilities. The
team leader should also number his people for control
purposes. This is usually done during the planning
phase. Numbering facilitates individual movement,
team movement, and the assembly of formations. Use
team formations continually in an effort to break the
habit of bunching up.

Wedge

The first tactical formation is the wedge (Figure 7).
The wedge formation provides good firepower to the
front, flanks, and rear, since all members can engage as
required. It enables the factors of speed, security, and

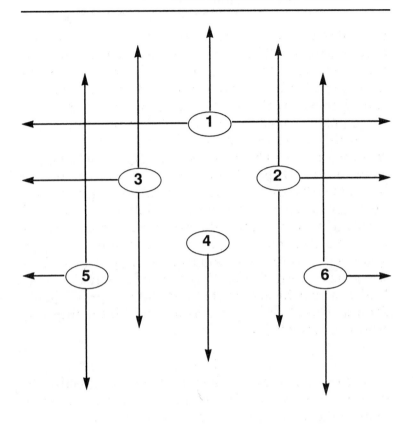

Figure 7: Wedge formation. The wedge formation provides the team members with the capability of firing to the front, flanks, and rear, providing 360-degree security. Speed, security, and control are fairly balanced. Use this formation whenever possible!

control to be exercised to a more even degree than any other formation. The team leader must ensure that the team members are separated enough to prevent any two from being hit by the same burst of fire and staggered enough to ensure that no more than two members are in the same line of adversary fire. This formation is also adaptable to team size as illustrated in Figure 8. Modifications can be made as required, as the wedge is easy to form or break down into other formations (Figures 9 through 9D). This formation requires odd-numbered members to form to the left and even-numbered members to form to the right. The formation is terrain sensitive, requiring fairly even ground and open space, and is very useful when crossing open areas. The wedge is fast-moving and easy to control by the team leader, who is located in the center of the formation. It should be used whenever possible, even if the threat of suspect contact is low.

File

The second formation the leader can choose is the file (Figure 10). This is easily remembered by the concept of "follow the leader" or "ducks in a row." It is fast-moving and hard to control, and security to the front and rear are poor. How many people can fire to the front or rear? One. Remember that friendly fire isn't friendly. If the operator in front kneels, the next operator shouldn't fire over his head, as he may stand up at any moment. Security on the flanks is strong. This formation is used in hallways, stairwells, alleys, dense terrain, darkness, or any place where space is limited.

Line

The third formation is the line (Figure 11). This formation provides maximum firepower to the front and rear. Flank security is poor—only one operator can fire on each flank. It is difficult to control, since everyone is

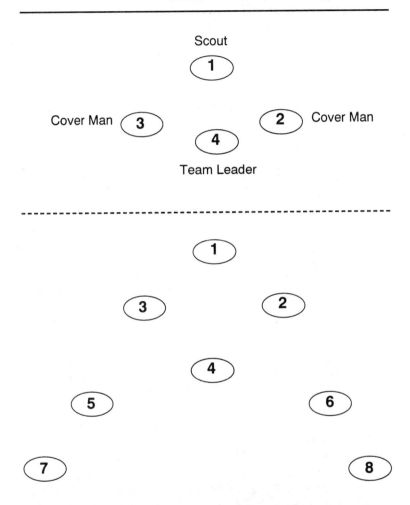

Figure 8 (upper): 4-man wedge. Either the #2 or #3 cover man can serve as rear security, or both can, depending on the tactical arena. The team leader is normally placed in the center of the formation for command and control purposes. He will fill in at any position as required.

Figure 8 (lower): 8-man wedge. #1 scout, #2 cover man, #3 cover man, #4 team leader, #5 cover man, #6 cover man, #7 assistant team leader, #8 rear security. The 8-man team is extremely strong and versatile. The team could run an extended point or two rear securities. The assistant team leader helps in command and control duties.

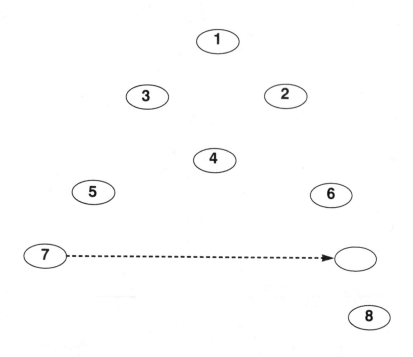

Figure 9: Heavy right wedge. The team leader in this case has identified a danger area to the right flank. To counter the situation he has shifted the #7 man to the right flank in order to enhance the firepower in that direction. More members can be shifted as required. A dual point could be chosen by bringing the #2 or #3 man into a flanking position next to the #1 man. Another point option is to extend the #1 man's position 25 to 50 meters, then place the #2 or #3 man 5 meters in front of the team in the second point position. A dual rear security option is available by adding the #7 man to this responsibility; no shifting is required. An extended rear security can be developed in reverse of the extended point procedure. Extend the #8 man's position 25 to 50 meters behind the team, then place the #7 man 5 meters behind the team. Danger areas are numerous; so are adaptations. This formation's flexibility is only limited by the team's imagination.

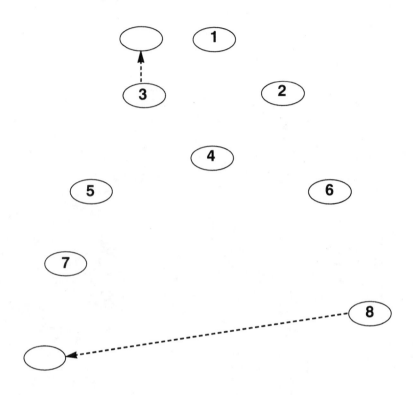

Figure 9A: Heavy left wedge. The team leader in this case has identified a danger area to the left flank. To counter the situation he has shifted the #8 man to the left flank in order to enhance firepower in that direction. More members can be shifted as required.

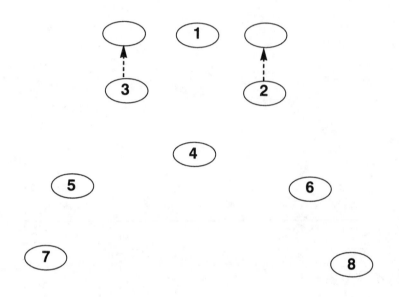

Figure 9B: Dual point. A dual point can be chosen by bringing the #2 or #3 man into a flanking position next to the #1 man.

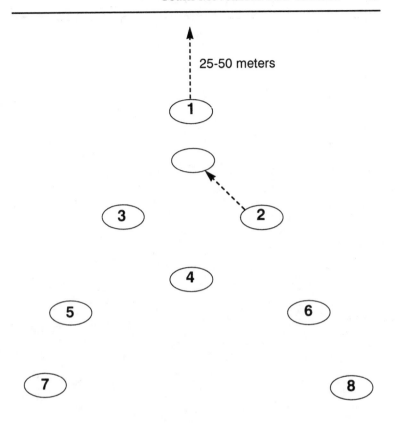

Figure 9C: Extended point. The extended point is accomplished by extending the #1 man 25 to 50 meters in front of the team, then moving the #2 man into the #1 man's former position.

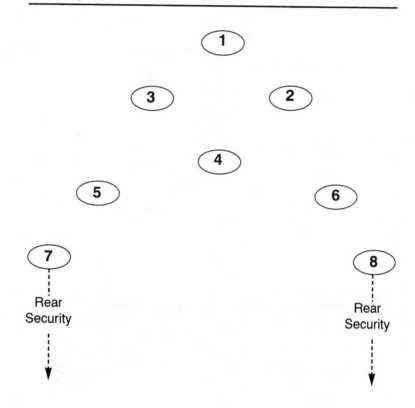

Figure 9D: Extended rear guard. The team leader has identified a danger area to the rear. A dual rear security option is available by adding the #7 man to this responsibility. No additional shifting is required.

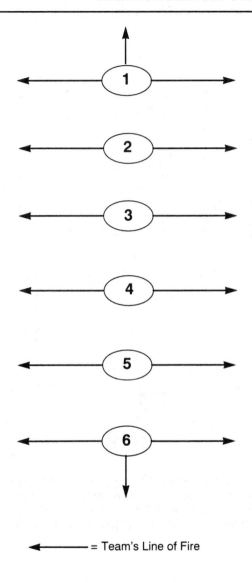

<———————— = Team's Line of Fire

Figure 10: File formation. Front and rear security are poor; only one member can safely fire in those directions. Flank security is strong; all members can safely fire in those directions. This formation is fast-moving and hard to control. Just follow the leader. Watch your interval. This formation is conducive to bunching up due to the habit of standing in line.

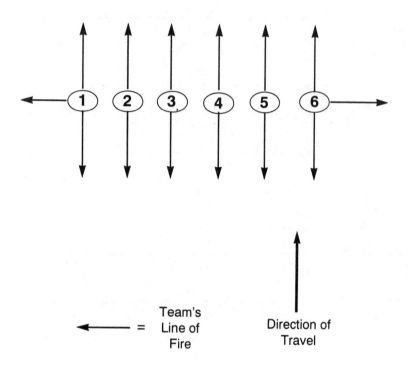

Team's
⟵——— =   Line of
Fire

↑
Direction of
Travel

Figure 11: Line formation. This formation provides the team with the ability to mass firepower to the front and rear. Flank security is poor; only one member can fire to a flank. This formation is difficult for the team leader to control and requires a great deal of space.

looking forward and must rely on their peripheral vision to stay on line. If an operator doesn't stay on line, he can stitch someone up the back or have this done to him. This formation is used to assault a position or to conduct sweeps/searches and clears. This formation also requires a great deal of space.

Column

The fourth basic formation is the column (Figure 12). The column is really a condensed wedge. If the team leader can't form a wedge, he should pick this formation if at all possible. It is fast-moving and fairly easy to control. It provides good security to the front, flanks, and rear. This formation is often used when following lightly armored vehicles or when using roads or large trails.

Stationary Formation: The Wagon Wheel

There is a formation the leader may choose when the teams aren't moving. These instances occur when listening, resting, rallying, surrounded, or disseminating information. It is the circle or wagon wheel (Figure 13). It provides 360-degree coverage, and control is easy to maintain. If the leader is issuing instructions, SWAT members must still face outward. Often operators will look at the leader when he is talking. Correct and avoid this tendency. The leader must always account for his members before resuming the operation.

TEAM MOVEMENT

After tactical formations have been decided upon by the team leader, he must decide which team movement is applicable. The indicator will be whether contact is unlikely, likely, or has been made. The team movement choices available are traveling, traveling overwatch, and bounding overwatch. The team leader may decide to utilize lightly armored vehicle techniques. Sound team

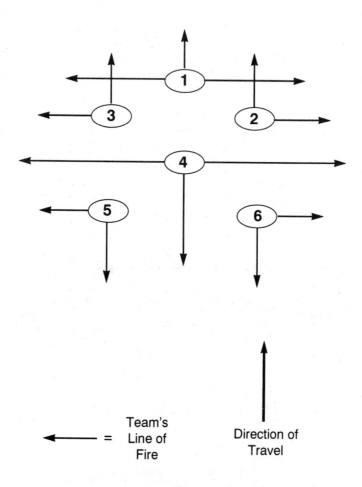

Team's Line of Fire

= Team's Line of Fire

Direction of Travel

Figure 12: Column formation. The column, a condensed wedge, possesses the same strengths as the wedge but not to as great an extent. This is due to the column's more condensed configuration. The formation is fairly fast-moving and easy to control. It is generally used when following vehicles on foot or when following roads or large trails. It is the second strongest formation after the wedge.

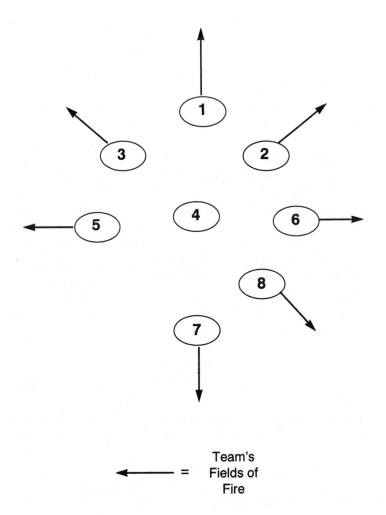

Team's
= Fields of
Fire

Figure 13: Wagon wheel formation. This formation is used for maximum protection when halted in the tactical arena. A 360-degree field of fire is set up. Each member drops to one knee at a minimum. Bullets are normally fired waist high and upward; the closer you are to the ground the better. Use this formation at listening halts, rally points, when surrounded, or to disseminate information.

movements utilize the SWAT team's inherent strength. Poor team movement breeds poor results.

Traveling/Traveling Overwatch

When contact is unlikely or when speed is chosen over security, traveling is used. During traveling, two separate units move at the same time along the same route. Distance, separation, and muzzle control must be maintained (Figure 14). Traveling overwatch is used when distance to the target is closed and contact is still unlikely; speed is chosen over security, but to a lesser extent. During traveling overwatch, two separate units move at the same time along different routes (Figure 14A). Separation is maintained to prevent both teams from coming under fire from the same suspect's location, but they are close enough to support each other by fire. This technique is fast-moving and easy to control by line of sight. However, it is vulnerable because both teams are moving at once.

Bounding Overwatch

When contact is likely and security is chosen over speed, bounding overwatch is used (Figure 15). During bounding overwatch only one team moves at a time, and usually each team chooses a slightly different route. When one team selects a good covered position and prepares a base of fire, the other team bounds forward to the next covered position. Once the bounding team has reached the next covered position, they take up overwatch while the rear team bounds forward. The distance traveled during each bound will depend on the terrain, available cover and concealment, and the ability of the overwatch team to provide a base of fire. This technique provides maximum security because one team is always under cover and ready to fire on any suspect that engages the other team.

Bounding overwatch is slow and difficult to control

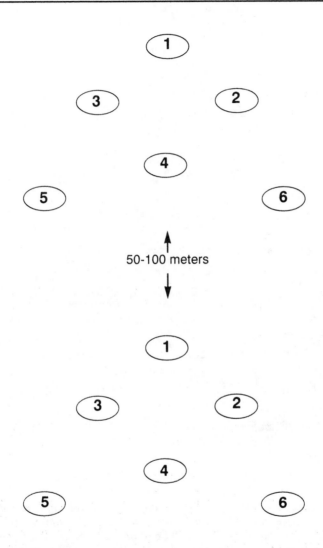

Figure 14: Traveling. When traveling, both teams move at the same time over the same terrain. Traveling is chosen for speed and should only be used when the expectations of contact are unlikely or low.

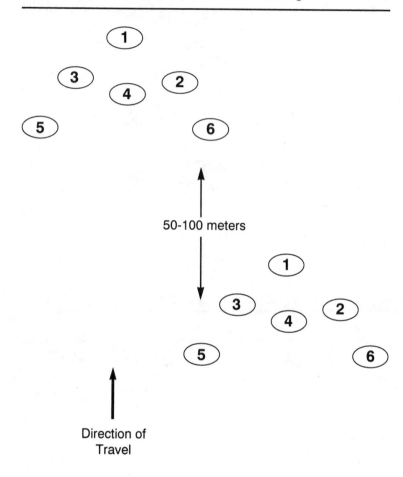

50-100 meters

Direction of
Travel

Figure 14A: Traveling overwatch. *During traveling overwatch, both teams are moving at the same time but over slightly different terrain. The following team will be to the flank of the lead team in order to react to adversary fire. At this time, the following or reserve team will maneuver aggressively to flank the adversary and extract the lead team from their situation. This technique is chosen for its speed.*

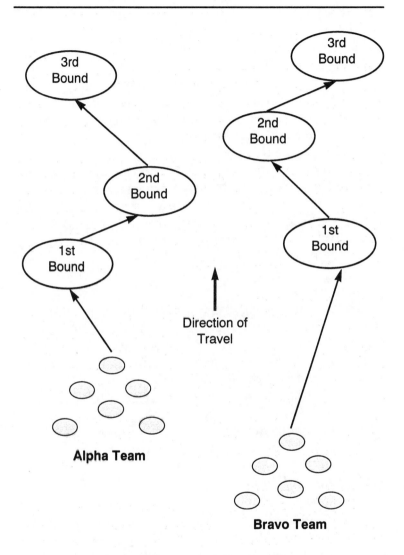

Figure 15: Bounding overwatch. In this situation, Alpha team, expecting contact, sets up in a sound tactical position. Bravo team then bounds to a sound tactical position. Alpha then bounds to their next position. Bounding continues, with the teams alternating the lead until no longer necessary. One team sets up a base of fire and the other moves.

since only one team moves at a time. The leader must take time to pick out the team's next covered position prior to moving. He must ensure his team doesn't cross into the cover team's field of fire. He must also account for all team members prior to moving. The bounding overwatch is loud and can be physically taxing, and a team shouldn't bound for more than five seconds. A good rifleman will index his target and fire in approximately five seconds. A phrase to run through the operator's mind to estimate an adversary's target acquisition and engagement time is, "He sees me, he aims, he fires"—the member should now be taking cover. Bounding overwatch can be performed either by leapfrogging or inchworming.

Leapfrog Technique

The first bounding overwatch technique is called the leapfrog (Figure 16). The leapfrog technique requires the bounding team to pass the overwatch team. The bounding team then takes up a new overwatch position to the front and flank of the initial overwatch team. The second team then bounds past the first, repeating the process as necessary. To easily remember the leapfrog process, think about mechanics—base of fire on flank, then change leads. Team one leads, then team two, etc.

Inchworm Technique

The second bounding overwatch technique is called the inchworm. The inchworm is chosen to keep the bases of fire closer together or when the terrain and visibility is working against the team. This technique requires the lead team to move forward under the cover of the trail team. They then take up a new overwatch position to provide a base of fire as the trail team catches up. The lead team will always be in the lead (Figure 17). It looks like an inchworm moving, hence the name.

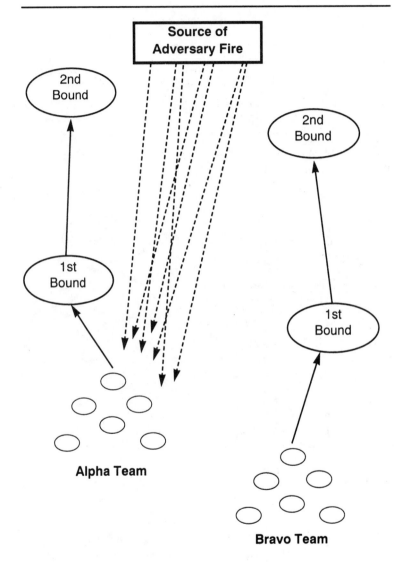

Figure 16: Leapfrog technique. In this situation, Alpha team returns fire and Bravo team immediately flanks right. Bravo team then sets up a base of fire. Alpha team then bounds to their next best position; in this case they are set up to assault the adversary's position. Bounding is complete at this point. Normally, when bounding, the teams alternate the lead. One team sets up a base of fire while the other moves or leapfrogs.

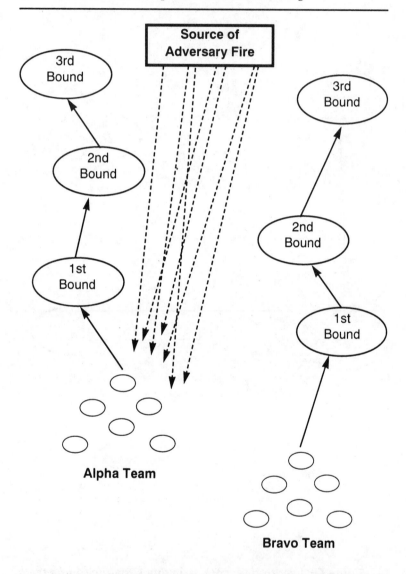

Figure 17: Inchworm technique. The inchworm method masses firepower by keeping the bases of fire close together. The lead team maintains the lead throughout the maneuver. Here, Alpha team makes contact; Bravo team flanks and sets up adjacent to Alpha team. Alpha bounds again and sets up, and Bravo bounds adjacent to Alpha. This is repeated as required.

TEAM MOVEMENT UNDER FIRE

The next decision the team leader has to make occurs when the team is under fire. Control is difficult at best, and unless the leader acts quickly and decisively, confusion and death will result. Normally, continued movement will be required to contain, dislodge, or eliminate the adversary.

There are three techniques of choice for team movement under fire: fire and maneuver, fire and movement, and assault fire. The technique chosen is determined by the cover available and the distance to the suspect.

Fire and Maneuver

The first technique is fire and maneuver, which is used upon initial contact, when the location of a suspect's fire is relatively distant and there is adequate cover and concealment for the maneuvering team (Figure 18). During fire and maneuver the whole team moves by bounding overwatch until they are relatively close to the adversary, run out of adequate cover and concealment, or the suspect can fire effectively on the team. Fire and movement is then employed.

Fire and Movement

During fire and movement, individual members of the team move rather than the whole team at once. The stationary members add their fire to that of the supporting team. The key to success is to maintain the heaviest volume of fire possible on the suspect to prevent him from firing effectively on the moving team member. Effective control of fire from both teams is essential. The ultimate situation is to flank the suspect's position, enabling effective team fire to be delivered from two or more positions (Figure 19). Keep track of the ammunition expenditure, and coordinate movement with reloading. Redistribute ammunition as required. The leader

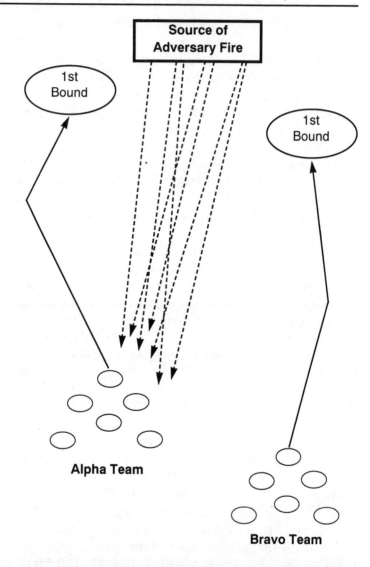

Figure 18: Fire and maneuver. During fire and maneuver, the whole team moves until they are close to the adversary, run out of cover and concealment, or the suspect fires effectively on the team. In this figure, Alpha and Bravo have bounded to positions where one team will maintain a base of fire and the other will assault, if required.

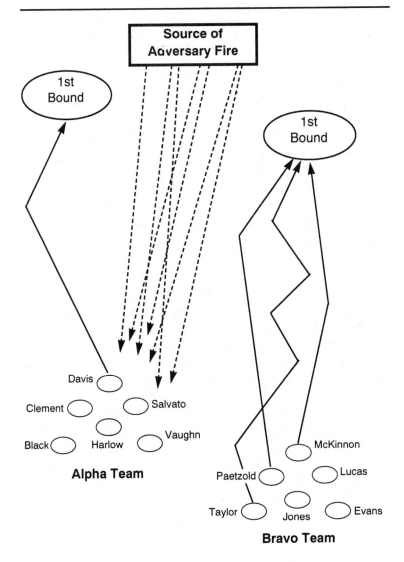

Figure 19: Fire and movement. During fire and movement, only certain members move instead of the whole team. Stationary members add their fire to the supporting team's fire. The team leader designates bounding members by name. In this example, Alpha team has a base of fire set up, so the Bravo team leader yells for McKinnon, Taylor, and Paetzold to move. The remaining members add their fire support to Alpha team's.

designates movement by radio, hand signal, or voice. He designates moving personnel by name or prior established number, such as, "McKinnon, Taylor, and Paetzold prepare to move—move!"

Often during planning, team members have been assigned numbers as designators for an assault. A 6-man team would be numbered one through six. The leader may use, "Numbers one, three, and five prepare to move—move!" Numbers two, four, and six are next. Another variation of the numerical method would be, "Odd numbers prepare to move—move!" Even numbers are next. This mixes members moving from random locations to avoid setting a pattern for suspect target acquisition.

Assault Fire

Assault fire is conducted by a team or designated members. This is used as a last resort when the responding team is extremely close to the suspects and there is no longer sufficient cover and concealment to allow members to move (Figure 20). This technique is difficult to control since the base-of-fire team leader must cease his team's fire prior to the assault fire team entering the suspect's position. If this is done prematurely, suppressive fire is lost. If tardy, friendly fire will ensue. The assault fire members enter the suspect's position, neutralize him, then set up security in case any other suspects have escaped. The overwatch teams move forward, implementing search and clear procedures to complete the security of the scene.

COORDINATED WEAPONS FIRE ON TARGET

To enable these techniques of movement under fire to work, the leader must get weapons fire on target. Be aware that not everyone will know where adversary fire is coming from. This may be due to the operator's posi-

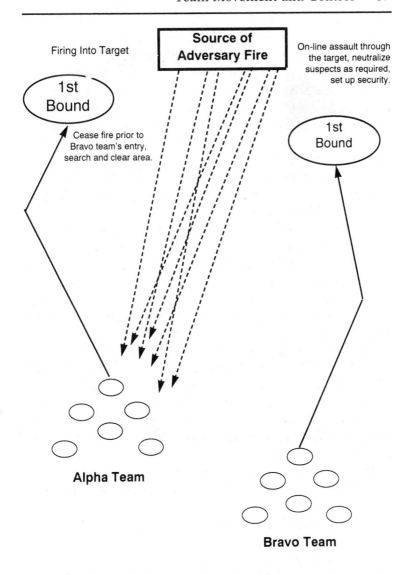

Figure 20: Assault fire technique. Alpha team lays down covering fire, Bravo team forms an on-line assault formation. Alpha team ceases fire prior to Bravo team's insertion into the affected area. Bravo team enters the area, neutralizing adversaries as required, then sets up security. Alpha team then enters the area performing search and clear procedures.

tion in the formation, confusion, surrounding conditions, distance, and echoing around built-up areas. When a team member identifies the suspect's firing position, he returns fire and yells the distance, clock reference, notable feature, and weapons system. A field expedient method to get fire on target is to utilize tracer rounds. The member yells, "Watch my tracer!" and then fires on the suspect's position (Figure 21).

The object is to get the maximum amount of coordinated, accurate suppressive fire on target as quickly as possible. The team leader can then choose the proper movement technique or break contact and continue the mission if a delaying action or diversion is suspected. He may choose a certain weapon to fire and tell others to hold their fire. For example, if the suspect is 100 yards away, the shotgun and handgun will not be very effective, so they hold fire until the team maneuvers closer. The team leader's fire command would be, "Seventy-five yards, one o'clock, building, rifleman, MP5s, M16s, semiautomatic—FIRE!" This concept does not condone indiscriminate weapons fire. Consider General Student's quote: "The most precious thing when in contact with the enemy is ammunition. He who fires uselessly, merely to assure himself, is a man of straw" (General Kurt Student, "Ten Commandments of Paratroopers," 1938). Be aware of your surroundings, and watch for innocent personnel in the area. SWAT operators are responsible for every round fired.

LIGHTLY ARMORED VEHICLES

A final technique requiring discussion is the employment of lightly armored vehicles. They can be used to assault a suspect's position, as a mobile base of fire, and as mobile cover and concealment. Team members may ride inside buttoned up or may follow behind. If teams follow behind, the team leader must have contact with the vehicle commander. If not, they may outrun the team.

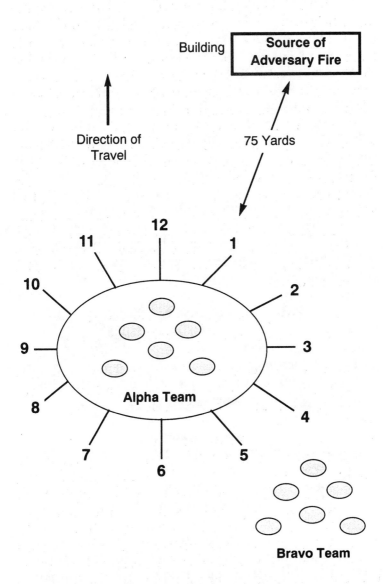

Figure 21: Getting fire on target. In this case, the point man identifies the source of fire by using a clock reference. He returns fire and yells, "Seventy-five yards, one o'clock, building, rifleman."

The pace is set by the ground team. It's not pleasant to move behind a vehicle wearing tactical gear and perhaps a gas mask, only to discover on the approach that the team can't keep up. The perception in the vehicle is that they are going slow when, in reality, they are running the team into the ground. Consider what 5 mph feels like in a vehicle and what it feels like on the ground dressed out.

Common sense dictates that the vehicle must be situated between the target and the assault team. However, the team leader must govern the direction of travel as well. Just remember that when rounds splash off or skip under the armor, the situation can turn stressful. Maintain control, follow the plan, and drive on. If casualties are sustained, halt the vehicle and put them inside. The vehicle can also be utilized for protection if a tactical withdrawal is necessary, such as to medevac a wounded man.

FREQUENTLY ENCOUNTERED TACTICAL CONDITIONS

There are a few conditions that SWAT teams encounter frequently, and their reactions to them can relate to the team's tactical effectiveness or survival.

Rooftop Travel

The first condition is when teams travel on rooftops. Do not skirt the edge; this will backlight the team, enabling a suspect to observe the movement from extremely long distances or even attract weapons fire. Travel as far as possible from the edge to prevent this. This is the same concept as observing the military crest of a hill, where you travel far enough below the hilltop to prevent backlighting. The human eye is attracted to movement and shape. If the team contrasts with the horizon, the chances of discovery are increased.

Road Crossing

Another frequently encountered condition is when SWAT teams cross a road. Cross at the military crest of a dip, if possible, or cross at a corner. This decreases a suspect's field of view or fire. A suspect can be expected to cover the long axis, hoping to observe or employ weapons on a team (Figure 22). Do not cross the road one member at a time, as this activity will heighten the adversary's chances of team discovery and target acquisition (like ducks in a shooting gallery). If one operator is spotted, the suspect will set up on the area hoping for another target of opportunity. Cross the road simultaneously; the adversary may see this, but the team will already be across, thus avoiding adversary fire.

Open Area Crossing

The next condition often experienced is crossing an open area, such as an open field. The first rule is to circumvent it if possible. If not, choose a good formation like the wedge. Next, observe the area before you initiate the crossing. Place your weapons in a manner so that their capabilities best fit the circumstance. Finally, move as quickly as possible across this area. A good formation that observes proper weapons placement enhances the team's survival.

Now is not the time to be conservative; choose speed. If you get caught in the open, the power curve has shifted to the adversary. Moving in any direction presents the adversary with ample targets. Going to the ground presents the adversary with stationary targets. The adversary will cover open areas in order to exploit the SWAT team's mistake (Figure 23).

Obstacle Breach

An additional condition is any type of breaching circumstance, such as fences, walls, terrain features, channeled areas, and obstructed areas. The rule of thumb is

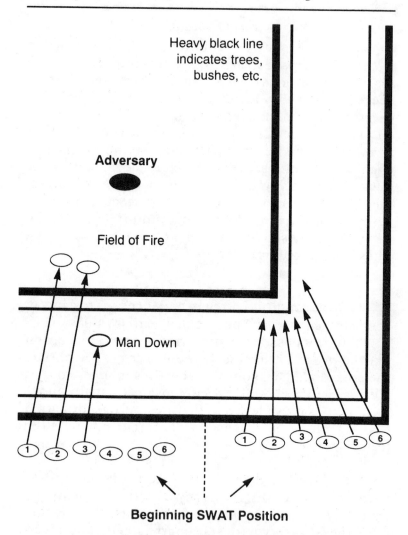

Beginning SWAT Position

Figure 22: Road crossing. At left, improper crossing on the long axis of the road—the team is split. Numbers 1 and 2 went to the far side of the road first, #3 is shot in the middle of the road, and numbers 4, 5, and 6 are stuck in their original positions. At right, the team performs a proper crossing at the corner. The suspect's field of fire is restricted on either axis. The line formation is correct. All team members cross at the same time instead of like ducks in a shooting gallery.

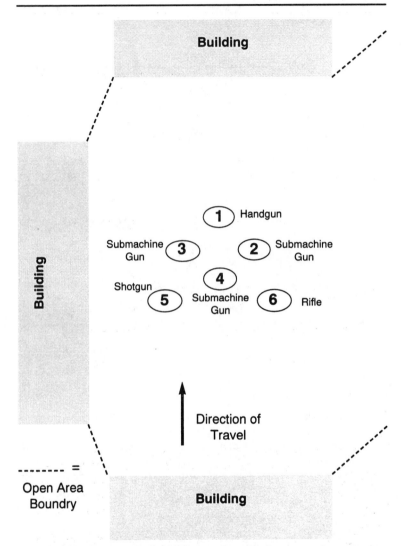

Figure 23: Crossing an open area. The team has chosen the strongest formation possible, the wedge. They have observed the area before committing. The weapons have been placed according to their unique effective envelopes. Now the team moves across the open area as quickly as possible. The team leader is monitoring control, security, and speed. If possible, a sniper team would be overwatching this area. If a weak formation was chosen, consider the devastation a team could suffer getting caught in the open.

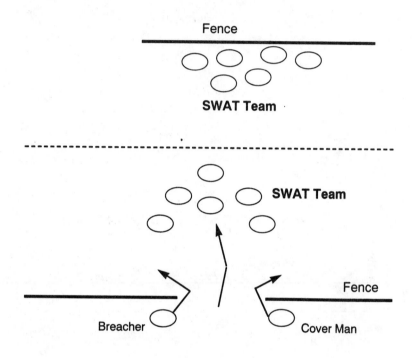

Figure 24 (upper): Improper fence breach. Adversaries will cover obstacles such as fences with weapons. This team has bunched up, losing security and control. It only takes one person to cut a fence or two to set up a fence assist, so why bring up the whole team? The whole team is now in danger instead of two men, whom the team could extricate if required.

Figure 24 (lower): Proper fence breach. Only two members were committed—the breacher and the cover man. The rest of the team remains in a covered and concealed position waiting for the breacher's signal. In this case the fence is cut, the breacher and the cover man move through the fence, hold it open, and the team moves through, forming a good tactical formation on the far side. When the team is through, the breacher and cover man integrate into the formation. This procedure exposes only two men, who can be helped by a strong team if trouble develops.

don't bunch up. Send at least one cover man and the necessary number of breachers, and maintain rear security. See Figure 24 for both a proper and improper fence breaching.

Dog Knot

A final often encountered circumstance is the dog knot. This bunching up occurs when dismounting vehicles, at listening halts, when receiving verbal information, before or after breaching an obstacle, and before moving into required formations. Always maintain a staggered configuration, observing separation and other security techniques. Keep weapons pointed outboard, and drop to one knee or prone out as required. Remember that humans travel erect, so rounds are normally fired waist high and up; stay as close to the ground as possible. There is no reason not to. This is a direct reflection of leader and team professionalism. Take nothing for granted; adhere to 360-degree security all of the time when in the tactical area of responsibility. Remember, the team is operating in a permissive environment open to danger from any direction at any time.

Chapter 4
TACTICAL PLANNING

Tactical planning is the most tedious aspect of any tactical operation, but it is perhaps the most critical. The leader will hear comments from SWAT operators stating that planning is nonessential or useless because no plan ever works as envisioned. These views are voiced by operators who are inadequately trained in tactical planning, misunderstand the value of planning, or have never had a "wing it" style operation go sour. It is guaranteed that even an incomplete, weak plan is better than no plan at all.

Tactical planning enables the team leader to make difficult tactical decisions in a more efficient manner. The plan is a dynamic concept assisting in team safety, jogging the team leader's memory, choosing logistics, ensuring that the mission is commensurate with the team's capabilities, lessening vicarious liability, delineating responsible entities, courtroom testimony, identifying tactical responsibilities, and fostering a can-do attitude. It is also a learning tool for future operations.

Tactical planning is not just a leadership task; it requires subordinate participation as well. The team leader cannot plan a whole operation by himself. If he tries, the chances of failure are high due to time constraints, information overload, and limited thinking. One man considering an operation will be limited to his personal mind-set and experience, but when the whole team participates the options are increased manyfold. Through team involvement, the plan takes on the identity of the team plan instead of the team leader's plan.

ANALYZE THE MISSION

To begin planning, the mission must be analyzed. All information available must be collected, such as containment information, Field Command Post (FCP) location, assessment information, and witness information. Analyze the terrain and target area. Develop possible courses of action (open-air assault, building assault, stealth or crisis entries, vehicle assault, or a combination of options). Determine special aspects and restrictions, such as the presence of children or older or ill hostages, use of force policies, rules of engagement (ROE), type and intent of suspect, and environmental, safety, and health constraints.

INITIAL TACTICAL ACTIONS

Initiate tactical actions adhering to departmental policy and procedure statements. Consider past operations. Consider resources available plus team capabilities and limitations. Send the scout/snipers out immediately to gather intelligence. Start interacting with the Tactical Operations Center as soon as practical.

WARNING ORDER

Next, write and issue the warning order. This order notifies the team of an impending mission and enables them to organize preparations for that mission. This order can be utilized as an emergency plan or to change and adjust to actions already occurring. These changes are placed into the warning order format and attached to the operations order. The warning order is actually a condensed operations order. It is also used as a reference when writing the operations order.

Warning Order Contents

A. SITUATION—Brief statement of the suspect and friendly situation.

B. MISSION—Who does what, where, when, and why.

C. GENERAL INSTRUCTIONS:

   1. General and special organization; tasks assigned to elements and teams.

   2. Uniform and equipment common to all.

   3. Weapons, ammunition, and equipment common to all, plus special weapons and equipment.

   4. Chain of command structured to the last man.

   5. Communications: cover hand signals, special means, channels.

   6. Time schedule: correct time, initial brief, final brief, inspection, insertion.

D. SPECIFIC INSTRUCTIONS—Issued to special purpose teams and key individuals.

Warning Order Example

A. SITUATION—On 4/30/95, at 0900 hours, a group of three armed men entered the Lotsa Money Credit Union located at First and Texas. The suspects are armed with two shotguns and one handgun. One security guard is dead, and hostages have been taken. Raw intelligence is validated by an employee who escaped the attempted robbery. A 360-degree cordon has been established, and the Field Command Post is operating out of Sparkle Cleaners located at Second and Texas.

B. MISSION—Bravo team assaults the Lotsa Money Credit Union at 0400 tomorrow to locate and apprehend the suspects following the departmental deadly force policy. Rescue and protect hostages. Resecure the scene.

[These statements have answered who, what, when, where, and why.]

C. GENERAL INSTRUCTIONS [how]:

1. General and special instructions:

   a. Alpha Team: Team leader tasks personnel for tactical planning and emergency entry duties. Alpha team will insert no later than 1200 hours, today's date, and set up on side four, opening one. Building assault will only occur upon compromise or command.

   b. Bravo Team: Team leader tasks personnel for tactical planning of crisis building entry and hostage rescue mission.

   c. Sniper/Scout Teams: Alpha, Bravo, Charlie, Delta. Immediate insertion for intelligence gathering, 360-degree deployment. Sniper leader covers setup location, rules of engagement, deadly force policy, phase lines, and compromise procedures.

2. Uniform and Equipment: Departmental specific, refer to standard operating procedures.

3. Weapons and Equipment: Organic to department. The team leader evaluates for the use of any special weapons or equipment.

4. Chain of Command: SWAT commander, sniper team leader, assault team leaders.

ALPHA TEAM HARLOW	BRAVO TEAM JONES
1. Salvato	1. McKinnon
2. Davis	2. Lucas
3. Vaughan	3. Evans
4. Clement	4. Cearley
5. Paetzold	5. Taylor
6. Truax	6. Finley
7. Griffiths	7. Minton

SNIPER TEAM BLACK

Alpha
1. Cockerham
2. Adkins

Bravo
1. Belknap
2. Foust

Charlie
1. Coburn
2. Douglas

Delta
1. Ephli
2. Houseman

5. Communications: Generic hand signals; refer to standard operating procedures. Utilize channel two. If adversary monitoring is suspected or jamming occurs, change to channel one.

6. Time Schedule:

   Current Time: The time is now 0930 hours.
   Initial Brief: 0945 hours
   Final Brief: 1015 hours
   Inspection: 1035 hours
   Sniper Insertion: 1040 hours
   Insert Alpha Team: 1100 hours
   Insert Bravo Team: 0400 hours, 5/1/95

D. SPECIFIC INSTRUCTIONS:

1. Detail personnel to obtain necessary equipment. Use spare officers for this; try not to tie up active operators on these tasks. The operators should be rehearsing their part of the tactical plan and be ready for insertion at a moment's notice.

2. Prepare team members for the mission. Cover any possible deviations such as secondary entry points. Rehearse the mission, then try alternate methods to discover additional possibilities. For example, rehearse a building search and clear, then run the rehearsal in reverse to identify strengths, weaknesses, or other possibilities.

3. Brief special purpose personnel or additional assets (explosive ordnance personnel, canine handlers, hostage handlers, arrest teams, trailers, evidence handlers, medical support, fire department, etc.).

BRIEFING

When briefing team members, use an authoritative, clear tone and direct operators to hold questions until the end of the briefing. This principle prevents disruptions in the continuity of the order. Make sure the warning order is understood, supervised, and accomplished. Once the operation is placed into motion, apply it through force, energy, and action in order to achieve surprise, speed, and violence of action. Remember, the warning order is an emergency plan spawned from initial information. It will only be implemented due to exigent circumstances. As the situation develops, information and support will be utilized to plan and implement a formal operations order. A formal tactical command structure should be utilized (Figure 25).

TACTICAL CHAIN OF COMMAND

At the top of the chain of command structure should be the members of the Emergency Operations Center. The EOC is staffed by top department officials or their delegates, such as the environmental safety and health representative, logistics representative, public relations representative, etc. Staffing is a departmental management function. Their mission is to manage and support the response to emergency situations, keeping required personnel informed about the status and plans for crisis resolution. The EOC approves the operations order unless compromise procedures are initiated. *Develop a signature block at the end of the operations order requiring the EOC commander to sign off on.* This provides the SWAT operators with some protection against management's propensity to lapse into selective memory should a mission go sour. The operator may find many career elitists filling positions in the EOC who have a habit of delegating authority and responsibility. These

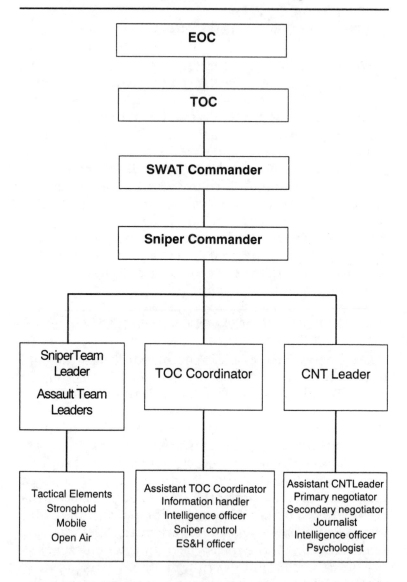

Figure 25: Formal tactical command structure.

individuals shouldn't be able to delegate responsibility, but depending upon the department's political atmosphere, it can be done. The EOC also coordinates the SWAT team leader's request for support or logistics, such as explosive ordnance disposal personnel, canine handlers, and lightly armored vehicles. Finally, the EOC maintains contact with other officials, the media, and the public as required.

Note: *The EOC is not a command and control element for SWAT teams operating in a tactical arena.* To clarify, the EOC approves and orders the mission but does not command and control SWAT team processes or tactics. Support is the key concept. The EOC may be established anywhere except near the crisis area or mixed in with the TOC. If the EOC is too near the crisis area, their ability to function will be curtailed. Also, if the EOC is set up in conjunction with the TOC, meddling, confusion, and disruption of operations will result.

TACTICAL OPERATIONS CENTER

The second entity in the chain of command is the Tactical Operations Center. It serves as a centralized location for all tactically significant information in support of the overall mission. The TOC is designed to capture, combine, and disseminate information to operational entities. This information is collected from witnesses, released hostages, captured suspects, sniper/scout team surveillance, crisis negotiations, technical surveillance, investigative follow-up procedures, and other actions. This all-source data supports investigative needs and operational planning.

Like the EOC, the TOC is not a command and control element. It is a mission support element. The TOC may be either mobile or static, but it is removed from the direct area of the target site. It must be close to the crisis negotiation team (CNT). The TOC may contain the

CNT if they are secluded. This enables expedient two-way communications. If the negotiators need information or gain information, the dissemination will be as close to real time as possible.

The TOC must be close to the assault team's rehearsal site as well. The reasoning is the same as for the crisis negotiators—expedience of communications.

The TOC must be secure and out of the public eye. Post security around the TOC to control unauthorized individuals. An access roster is convenient to prevent misunderstandings. The TOC must not be located in the EOC or Field Command Post.

The TOC is staffed by:

A. TOC COORDINATOR—Coordinates TOC activities, directs information posting, identifies essential information for dissemination, and interacts with the SWAT commander.

B. ASSISTANT TOC COORDINATOR—Assists TOC coordinator and takes charge of his duties as required.

C. INFORMATION HANDLER—Posts in a timely manner all categorized information. Disseminates information between TOC sections.

D. INTELLIGENCE OFFICER—Handles all up-channel and down-channel intelligence information.

E. SNIPER CONTROL—Monitors sniper/scout activity. Plots their location depicting fields of view and fields of fire. Gathers and reports requested intelligence information. Develops suspect's pattern analysis. Ensures ultimate target coverage; assigns and numbers targets. Approves rules of engagement and compromise authority constraints. Assists the sniper leader as required.

F. CRISIS NEGOTIATION TEAM—Negotiates with the suspects. Monitors demands for transportation, food, money, press coverage, etc. The CNT monitors the delivery of all demands and attempts to control time constraints by steering unrealistic demands into realistic constraints. All negotiated actions must be coordinated with the SWAT operators. Hostage release is negotiated in such a manner as to ensure time and location of release. The CNT also attempts to drive tactical option constraints. For example, if a vehicle is negotiated for, the SWAT team should establish the vehicle constraints and position of delivery in order to achieve a successful vehicle assault. The CNT should be SWAT trained in order to avoid making poor tactical concessions. SWAT training also heightens proficiency in recognizing tactically significant information.

G. ENVIRONMENT, SAFETY, AND HEALTH OFFICER—As required if hazardous material is present or suspected.

The TOC is vital when planning past the warning order stage, since the operations order is information dependent. (See Figures 26 and 27.) All operational members are welcomed in the TOC. In fact, it should be mandatory that they view the information display periodically in order to foster ideas or answer questions. Information importance was best stated by the son of an Argentine doctor, guerrilla leader Ernesto "Che" Guevara, in a 1963 memorandum: "Nothing helps a fighting force more than current information. Moreover, it should be in perfect order, and done with capable personnel."

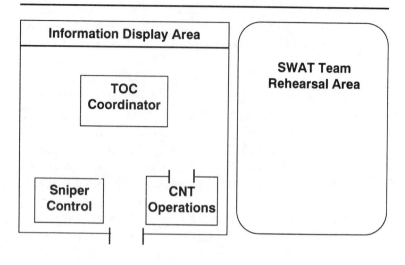

Figure 26: TOC layout.

FIELD COMMAND POST

The Field Command Post is not a direct entity operating in the tactical command structure; it operates in an attached function. The FCP is used to maintain cordon operations and to provide tactical support as required. Duties of the FCP include control of pedestrian/vehicle traffic, prevention of suspect escape, controlling media access, and the purging of adjoining buildings located in the tactical arena. The Golden Rule for cordon elements is *never shoot out of the target building once assault teams have initiated their mission.* Also, assault teams *never shoot out of the target building during their operation.* This prevents friendly fire incidences. The FCP must be notified of all tactical movements and decisions impacting their operations.

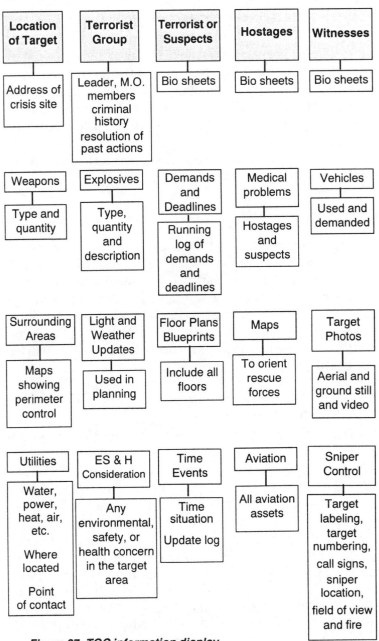

Figure 27: TOC information display.

SWAT COMMANDER

The third entity in the tactical command structure is the SWAT commander. He oversees the TOC and is primarily responsible for the successful resolution of the tactical situation. He is the primary link between the EOC and TOC. The SWAT commander participates in mission planning and briefs teams about their mission. He assists the assault team leaders, sniper team leader, TOC coordinator, and the CNT leader.

SNIPER COMMANDER

The fourth layer in the hierarchy is the sniper commander. He oversees the sniper leader and sniper teams. He gathers and disseminates information, plots sniper positions, monitors and records their radio traffic, designates fields of fire, authorizes position changes, develops suspect pattern analyses, initiates ROE (rules of engagement) changes, and labels and assigns targets. He works hand and glove with the sniper leader.

FIRST-LINE SUPERVISORS

The fifth layer of the command structure is composed of assault team leaders, the sniper team leader, the TOC coordinator, and the CNT leader. The assault team leaders are responsible for planning, briefing their team, and the successful accomplishment of their assigned mission. The sniper leader is responsible for planning, briefing the teams, controlling the teams, and the successful accomplishment of their assigned mission. The TOC coordinator is responsible for the overall functioning of the TOC and the successful accomplishment of the assigned mission. The CNT leader is responsible for planning, briefing his team and SWAT commander, plus the successful accomplishment of the assigned mission. All first-line supervisors are responsible for the welfare of their people (food, water, rotation, relief schedules, etc.).

OPERATIONAL ENTITIES

The final layer of the command structure are operational entities: SWAT operators, TOC operators, and CNT operators. SWAT operators are responsible for stronghold assaults, vehicle assaults, open-air assaults, hostage rescue, and tactical deliveries. TOC operators staff the TOC as assistant coordinators, information handlers, intelligence officers, sniper control, and ES&H officers. CNT operators staff the TOC as assistant CNT leaders, primary negotiators, secondary negotiators, journalists, intelligence officers, and psychologists. Each operator is responsible for the successful accomplishment of his assigned duties.

INFORMATION-GATHERING METHODS

Now that the warning order has been completed and issued, the EOC is operational, and the TOC is operational, operations order mechanics begin. Remember, the TOC will contain or can obtain required tactical information. Information-gathering methods are diverse and unique in each operation. Generally, the methods consist of:

1. Reconnaissance and surveillance—Observe the tactical arena and target from as many angles and heights as possible. One view may reveal what another cannot. Snipers/scouts are excellent sources of ground-level and elevated information.

    Air assets are valuable if available. Make maximum use of photography, video, and sketches. Remember Patton's advice: "You can never do too much reconnaissance" (Gen. George S. Patton, *War As I Knew It*, 1947).

2. Interrogation and debriefing—Sources are released hostages, captured suspects, friends and relatives of hostages, or friends and relatives of suspects. Do not debrief or interrogate these personnel inside the TOC—for security reasons, select a spot that is safe, secure, and private. Anyone who may see or hear sensitive information can compromise you. Once these individuals are released, they may compromise the TOC's location or SWAT operation.

3. Records—Of hostages and suspects (personal, medical, school, military, etc.). Try to obtain up-to-date pictures.

4. Documents—Analyze all notes and messages obtained from hostages and suspects.

5. Technical intelligence—Inspect all associated evidence. Follow all departmental evidence handling procedures.

6. Maps, photographs, terrain models, similar buildings or residences—Develop a map of the hostage site and surrounding tactical arena, including photographs of same. Obtain floor plans of the hostage site and adjacent buildings. Question building managers, workers, custodians, etc., to verify floor plan accuracy.

    If possible, develop a three-dimensional model of the site (wooden models, tape models, rope models, or sand tables). Build the model to scale for team rehearsals and the identification of danger areas. The target model also enhances the team's ability to choose primary and secondary entry points. Be as accurate as possible, even inserting furniture. Pay particular attention to possible hostage location, suspect location, suspect observation points, means of approach and escape, high-speed avenues of approach, dead space key terrain, door construction, danger areas, and door swing. Identify the location of light switches, emergency lights, security alarms, fire suppression systems, watchdogs, utilities, telephones, and intercoms. Note the sizes of hallways and rooms.

Pay particular attention to stairwell construction and type. Consider alternate access and observation points such as air conditioning ducts, elevators, light shafts, vents, and adjoining rooms.

7. Weather—Keep up-to-date weather conditions and forecasts posted. These conditions affect planning for clothing, water, and tactical decisions. For example, light rain or fog cuts down on noise; thunder provides ambient noise, enabling easier team movement; the lack of moonlight enables more efficient night maneuvers; etc.

8. Communications—Shut off the suspect's telephones in order to prevent the calling of adversarial reinforcement or talking to the media, etc. Establish your own controlled line for negotiations. Ensure communications have been established with the Field Command Post for cordon efficiency.

9. All source intelligence—Exploit all intelligence-gathering capabilities and additional lawful sources.

10. Clandestine listening devices—Use lawful devices but beware of adversary discovery; he may disseminate bogus information.

11. Counterintelligence—Allow the suspect access to bogus information.

HOSTAGE, SUSPECT, AND
TEAM CONSIDERATIONS

As the intelligence gathering begins, the SWAT team must consider certain aspects pertaining to the hostages, suspects, and the team itself.

A. HOSTAGES:

1. Obtain a detailed description to facilitate target identification.

2. How many are there? This is used to plan hostage handlers and the hostage handling area. Suspects may attempt to mix with hostages in an effort to escape or kill. Handcuff, search, account for, and identify everyone. Look for hostages who act nervous around one of their own.

3. Who are the hostages? People of importance, members of a certain organization or political faction, etc.

4. What are the hostages' names?

5. What are their mental and physical states? Are they mentally challenged, ill, or injured? Consider the Stockholm syndrome. This occurs when a hostage develops empathy toward a suspect; they may even help the suspect.

6. What are they wearing? Beware of suspects who may change clothes with hostages. Never use clothing as a target identifier.

7. What is their exact physical location? Begin the assault as close to the hostages as possible. The quicker the operators engage the suspects, the

more hostages they will save. If operators can circumvent suspects not guarding hostages, so much the better. Operators can always search and clear after the rescue.

8. What supplies are available to them? Food, water, first aid, creature comforts, etc.

B. SUSPECTS:

1. Obtain a detailed description to facilitate target identification.

2. How many are there? This factor is used to plan the minimum strength envelope. The standard formula is two SWAT operators to every one suspect. This formula is also used to plan arrest team support. Again, watch for suspects attempting to mix in with hostages.

3. Who are the suspects (criminal, mentally challenged, or terrorists)?

   a. Criminal—They are usually caught in a criminal act, so they will not have a plan for hostages. They probably will not take any unnecessary risks and will avoid physical contact with the police. They are receptive to negotiation efforts.

   b. Mentally challenged—They are hard to negotiate with and unpredictable. Their planning and tactical skills are usually weak.

   c. Terrorist—They will probably take great personal risks and have strong tactical skills and a plan. They may deliberately engage police forces and are prone to killing hostages to gain recognition. Oftentimes their goal is to destroy and kill for the purposes of publicity. Expect unusual tactics.

4.   What are the suspects' names (formal, informal, nicknames, aliases)?

5.   What is their mental and physical state (mentally challenged, overly adversarial, scared, ill, wounded, using drugs or alcohol, etc.)?

6.   What are they wearing? Remember the clothes-changing tactic.

7.   How are they armed? This identifies their firepower capabilities. Your approach is different when a suspect has a .38 snubnose in lieu of a semiautomatic rifle. The weapons platform defines fields of fire and range.

8.   What are their intentions, motivations, and demands?

9.   What are their strengths and weaknesses? Do they control the key terrain, or can SWAT teams obtain it? Do they have weak or strong firepower capabilities? Do they possess special equipment such as gas masks, etc.?

10.   Do they belong to civilian, military, or social organizations? If so, what are their philosophies?

11.   Are they present or former members of the above organization? If they are outcasts, perhaps present members will be willing to inform on them.

12. What methods of operation have been used by their organization in the past (destruction, killings, and/or hostage-taking)? What were the outcomes (surrender, suicide, fight to the death, etc.)?

13. What are the short-term objectives of the organization (destruction, death, political statement, blackmail, publicity, etc.)?

14. Does the parent organization support them, and do they support the goals of the organization?

15. Are there any local, national, or international personnel or organizations sympathetic to their actions? Look for possible support, reinforcement, or copycat actions.

16. How are they equipped (explosives, weapons, ammunition, gas masks, night vision devices, body armor, early warning devices, etc.)?

17. What means of communication is available to them (telephones, radios, television, monitoring devices, etc.)?

18. What supplies are available to them (food, water, first aid, etc.)?

19. Are there identified patterns of sleeping, eating, or guard duty? These patterns can indicate military training.

20. What is their reaction to negotiations?

21. What is their reaction to deliveries?

22. What are their probable locations?

23. Visualize what you believe the suspects' field of view would be from their vantage point.

24. Try to think like the suspects in order to counter their actions and predict their locations.

C. SWAT TEAM:

1. What is the mission? Remember, the mission must be commensurate with the SWAT team's strength and training. If the SWAT team overextends itself, disaster may result.

2. Has communication been established between all entities and the suspects? The EOC, TOC, Field Command Post, and any additional assets.

3. Are detailed physical layouts of the target area available (maps, video, photographs, blueprints, sketches, etc.)?

4. What are the best approach and withdrawal routes (primary and secondary)? Are there any high-speed avenues of approach?

5. What type of transportation should be utilized (on foot, soft units, lightly armored vehicles, air assists, etc.)?

6. Are there any danger areas (suspect-dominated key terrain, minimal cover or concealment, open areas, channeled areas, etc.)?

7. Are there snipers in the area or trailers setting up possible ambushes? Consider countersnipers, scheme of maneuver, tactical formation, and immediate-action drills.

8. What additional support is available (ambulance, life flight, fire department, arrest teams, hostage handlers, evidence protection team, bomb technician, etc.)?

9. Can pyrotechnics be used? Are there environmental, health, fire, or contamination concerns?

10. What diversions could be used (bullhorns, distraction devices, hailing systems, lights, phone calls, intercom systems, smoke/fire alarms, security alarms, intermittent building utilities cessation and restoration, etc.)?

In this case, the warning order has been issued. The sniper/scout teams and emergency building assault team are in place. The EOC and TOC are operational. The tactical arena and target have been reconned by sniper/scouts noting observation, key terrain, obstacles, cover and concealment, and avenues of approach and escape. The mission has been analyzed and a course of action chosen. The course of action in this case is building assault, crisis style. The second and third courses of action are open-air assault in conjunction with a vehicle assault. The next step is to plan the operations order.

OPERATIONS ORDER

There are many methods utilized by different agencies to plan the operations order. I think the five-paragraph military operations order is the most efficient. Consider all of the operations the various military branches have planned from small unit actions to large-scale battles. The effectiveness is apparent. To assist in remembering the five paragraphs in proper sequence, use the acronym SMEAC: 1) Situation, 2) Mission, 3) Execution, 4) Administration and logistics, and 5) Command and signals.

Using the warning order as a framework, the team begins writing the operations order. Note: *this is a team effort.* An efficient way to write the operations order is to divide each paragraph between two or three team members for completion. This enables all team members to participate, heightening their understanding of the overall mission, team tasks, and individual tasks. The plan will be completed much faster, and a feeling of concerted effort will exist.

A. SITUATION—in this paragraph address:

Adversary Forces—How many, location, type of equipment/weapons, status, and probable courses of action.

Friendly Forces—All forces supporting mission: EOC, TOC, medical, fire department, arrest teams, stay-behind security, hostage handlers, evidence handlers, canine units, explosive ordnance technicians, etc. Don't forget to coordinate team activities with them!

Attachments and Detachments—Any special-purpose equipment or personnel other than what the team originally operates with, i.e., life flight, explosives breaching, special ammunition, etc.

B. MISSION—in this paragraph address:

In plain, simple words exactly what the task is going to be. Cover WHO, does WHAT, WHEN, and WHERE. If possible, answer WHY. The WHY personalizes the mission. Team members like to know why their lives are being placed in jeopardy. The WHY portion also fosters a higher degree of commitment.

C. EXECUTION—in this paragraph address:

A step-by-step scheme of maneuver beginning at the line of departure (LOD) to the mission debrief. This paragraph is the most time-consuming and is the heart of the operations order. It is focused on HOW the mission will be accomplished. First, develop a statement delineating the general plan to be used to accomplish the mission. Next, address sub-unit tasks. Sub-units are team and individual tasks. Team tasks depict the manner by which each team will accomplish their designated tasks. Emphasis is placed on detail, compromise procedures, and contingency plans. Establish a line of compromised authority and ensure that it is understood by all operators and entities. The line of compromised authority is an area recognized as being so close to the target area that withdrawal will be dangerous and remaining in place will heighten the likelihood of discovery. *This is the point of no return.* When the line of compromised authority is reached, command and control automatically revert to the team leader. At this time, the team leader will say three times, "I AM IN CHARGE" (to ensure understanding), then set the plan into motion. Each team will attach their plan to the master operations order. A great deal of effectiveness will be lost if one entity attempts to plan every tactical entity's execution. Possible tactical team taskings are vehicle assaulters, open-air assaulters, building assaulters, etc.

After team actions are planned, address individual tasks. These tasks identify each specific individual task, i.e., designated shooter, hostage handler, gas man, grenadier, long rifleman, rear security, point, entry man, breacher, team assister, etc. Be sure to cover the deadly force policy, rules of engagement, rehearsal of operations, departure time hack, staging time hack, order of movement, routes to be followed, danger areas, phase lines, compromise procedures, post operation procedures, evaluation procedures, and debriefing location.

Finally, coordinate instructions with everyone essential to the mission. For example, if you need the containment forces on side four to deploy a distraction device at 0900 hours as a diversion, coordinate the delivery of the device, and make sure the time of implementation is understood as well as the mechanics of deploying the device. If other law enforcement agencies will be utilized, establish a means to identify them. Their danger may be heightened as they maneuver through the tactical arena due to their being equipped differently than the primary organization. All participants must know the identifier that marks them as friendly, such as tape, vest, arm bands, baseball caps, etc.

Remember, *friendly fire isn't friendly.*

D. ADMINISTRATION AND LOGISTICS—in this paragraph address:

All equipment required and direct personnel to obtain it. If the team leader can avoid it, he shouldn't assign team members logistical tasks. This will only tie them up when they need to be planning and rehearsing their team and individual tasks. Assign nonoperators to do this. Remember to tell them what to draw, how much to draw, and where to draw it. Administration and logistics will be decided upon in the execution section of the operations order. If bolt cutters or distraction devices are planned for in the execution paragraph, this is where they will be listed.

Some example categories are:

1. *Weapons and Ammunition*—Naturally, the planner will state the normal tactical ammunition load and generic weapons used in reference to the SWAT team's standard operating procedure. This saves time. Next, cover special weapons and ammunition not normally carried by the team but planned for in this particular operation. For example, four suppressed submachine guns, six 12-gauge breaching rounds, etc.

2. *Clothing and Equipment*—Once again refer to the SWAT team's SOP. State clothing and equipment that may be required to accomplish a specific task, i.e., Nomex hood and Nomex gloves for deploying distraction devices. Also, check the weather forecast (located in the TOC); operators need to dress for the conditions. Remember, the SWAT team may need to carry a large amount of gear to begin with, but as they use it and no longer need it, they dump it. (They can recover it later.) Bolt cutters swinging from a load-bearing harness or sticking out of a tactical vest will not be a welcome appendage when the operator is engaged in a crisis entry search-and-clear operation. Common sense dictates that operators cannot dump weapons, pyrotechnics, or anything that may be used against them.

3. *Special Equipment*—A statement covering equipment of a nonpersonal nature such as perimeter lights, cameras, and binoculars.

4. *Transportation*—A statement setting forth vehicle or other types of transportation requirements, such as soft units, lightly armored vehicles, and a SWAT van. Also, establish load plans, i.e., the order in which the team members will sit in order to facilitate off-loading into an effective tactical formation.

5. *Handling of Injured*—Written procedures for handling injured personnel, which includes hospital notification and ambulance or life flight standby. This is self-assuring for the team and shows compassion for the hostages as well as suspects. This is important in the courtroom.

6. *Handling of Suspects*—This is a statement covering the handling of prisoners, arrest team procedures, and transportation.

7. *Handling of Hostages*—This is a statement covering the hostage handling area, hostage handling procedures, and transportation.

8. *Handling of Evidence*—This is a statement of procedures for the evidence handling team covering the collection and preservation of evidence.

The aforementioned categories are subject to change with each tactical operation. Time-saving and efficiency will be realized through the use of standard operating procedures. (See Figure 28.) The development of SOPs is time consuming, but once completed they are invaluable in saving time during the operations order development. SOPs also prevent the problem of searching for standard operational gear, and they prevent memory lapses. SOPs are also used to direct established departmental procedures, such as evidence handling, use of force, and arrest procedures.

E. COMMAND AND SIGNALS—Each entity will establish a chain of command all the way down to the last man. This prevents team freeze-up or confusion if the only identified leader is taken out. This also prevents bickering between team members about who is in charge. The chain of command enables a quick, smooth, orderly transition of leadership tasks.

(1) *The vest will be stored in the SWAT equipment room located in the X-104 building, room #6.*

(2) *The vest will be hung on a clothing rack according to size: small, medium, large, extra large.*

(3) *30-round capacity M16 magazines will be placed in the four magazine pouches with the bullets to the bottom and pointing in toward the zipper. The magazines will be loaded with 28 rounds each for a total of 112 rounds.*

(4) *Battle dressing, one each, will be stored in the right chest pouch.*

(5) *The portable encrypted radio will be carried in the left chest pouch.*

(6) *The protection mask will be carried, prefitted, face-up, in the shoulder bag.*

The process continues until all standard equipment for this platform is covered. A diagram can be made if necessary.

Figure 28: SOP #1. Tactical vest set-up (M16 platform).

All team members must be briefed and aware of this procedure. *Do not establish the chain of command by seniority alone!*

Next, determine if clear voice or encrypted radio transmissions will be used. Establish a primary frequency and a secondary frequency in the event of suspect jamming, deception, or undesirable monitoring. Refresh team members on the use of hand and arm signals. Be sure to cover any unique hand and arm signals developed for a specific circumstance. Establish and brief team members on codes, sign/countersign procedures, duress words, authenticators, etc. Finally, cover special communication methods and their meaning, such as three whistle blows mean assault. These methods are used in the event radio contact is lost. They include but are not limited to whistles, horns, distraction devices, lights, bells, sirens, mirrors, smoke, bullhorns, public address systems, and flags (Figure 29).

SITUATION: Cover adversary forces, friendly forces, detachments, and attachments. _____

_____

MISSION: One paragraph stating who does what, when, and where. Answer why if applicable.

_____

_____

_____

EXECUTION: The heart of the plan. Cover team and individual tasks from the beginning of the mission to the end. How is stated here.

_____

_____

ADMINISTRATION AND LOGISTICS: Service and support. The identification, request, and procurement of all mission-essential equipment.

_____

_____

COMMAND AND SIGNALS: Chain of command to the last team member. Radio type, plus primary and secondary channels. Call signs and compromise procedures. Hand signals, special signals, etc.

_____

_____

EOC COMMANDER:_____Date:_____Time:_____
TOC COMMANDER: _____Date:_____Time:_____
SWAT COMMANDER: _____Date:_____Time:_____
TEAM LEADER:_____Date:_____Time:_____

Require any officer who is responsible for ordering the initiation of a mission and key entities to read and sign the operations order! Produce ample copies in order to prevent the "lost plan syndrome."

Figure 29: Operations order outline.

WARNING ORDER AND
OPERATIONS ORDER DIFFERENCES

The differences between the warning order and operations order should now be apparent. The warning order is a condensed plan suffering from lack of information and the need for expedient tactical action. Preparation of a warning order may have to be completed in as little as one hour. Remember, the warning order is used as a prelude to the operations order, as an emergency plan, or to implement required changes.

The operations order is time and information dependent. The operations order may take from one day to weeks to complete. This plan is the concerted effort of all responsible tactical entities and operators. The operations order mechanics must be understood, supervised, rehearsed, accomplished, and then debriefed. It must be flexible and dynamic. As each new bit of tactical information is identified, evaluate it, then decide if a tactical technique or procedure must be changed. It is understood that no operation goes exactly as planned. But as the planners trim simple-wild-ass-guess (SWAG) factors, mission success will be heightened. Plan from the beginning to the end of the mission, then implement the operation utilizing speed, surprise, and required violence of action.

DEBRIEF

The final aspect of tactical planning is a detailed debrief focusing on all aspects of the mission. All tactical entities should be involved. Each aspect of the mission is evaluated for effectiveness and improvement. The debrief topics include:

1. COMMAND, CONTROL, & COMMUNICATION (C3)—Was the chain of command efficient, clearly defined, and operational? Was the mission controlled

and coordinated effectively? Were all utilized communication procedures effective?

2. INTELLIGENCE AND TOC COORDINATION—Were intelligence-gathering methods useful and productive? Was the intelligence gathered identified by importance and posted expeditiously as well as correctly in the TOC?

3. SCHEME OF MANEUVER—Was the team's movement from the staging area through the approach to the final assault point secure and coordinated, and did it contain a proper balance between control, security, and speed? Were danger areas or obstacles breached effectively? Were phase lines utilized effectively? Was team compromise avoided?

4. OPERATIONAL PLANNING—Was operational planning complete, adhered to, and effective?

5. INDIVIDUAL ENGAGEMENTS, ROUNDS FIRED, LIGHTING CONDITIONS, VISIBILITY IMPROVEMENTS—Who did what? Who engaged what suspect where? How many rounds were fired and why? Was target identification difficult due to darkness, smoke, gas, or protective mask usage?

6. STATUS CHECKS REGARDING FINAL POSITIONS, HOSTAGES, SUSPECTS, AND ASSAULTERS—Did the team leader develop and utilize a status check procedure to assess the situation?

7. EXTRACTION PLAN, HOSTAGE HANDLING AREA, ARREST TEAMS, AND EVIDENCE HANDLERS—Was the extraction of hostages, suspects, and SWAT teams secure and efficient? Was evidence protected correctly?

8. SNIPER PLAN—Was the sniper plan efficient and coordinated correctly with other tactical entities and the TOC?

9. ADMINISTRATION AND LOGISTICS—Was the identification, planning, and gathering of logistics efficient?

10. COORDINATION WITH EXTERNAL AGENCIES—Was identification, utilization, and coordination with attached supporting agencies effective?

The debrief is not to be used as a finger-pointing session. The goal is to identify the tactical operation's strengths and weaknesses in order to utilize or avoid these conditions in future missions.

MISSION SUCCESS

What is mission success? This is a difficult question answered through personal philosophy. Is there a balanced formula concentrating on rescued personnel versus killed personnel, not to mention property damaged? Do you destroy the village to save the village, so to speak? There are recent law enforcement examples typifying this concept.

First, there are no acceptable losses in SWAT planning. I doubt if anyone remembers agreeing to die for a citizen. Remember that SWAT is a paramilitary organization, not a military organization. Soldiers are expected to die for their country, if required. If 10,000 soldiers are involved in a battle with an acceptable loss of 15 percent, that doesn't sound too bad as the soldier visualizes a sea of faces. But put this in respect to the team—eight operators who expect 15 percent losses. I hope the leader identifies a problem here, not only with philosophy but with performance.

Second, it must be understood that in most multiple hostage/suspect situations, the probability of losing a hostage is high. Where is the line between success and failure drawn? If you have ten hostages and only four are saved, is this a success? In my view, yes, because all ten were at the mercy of the suspects, therefore four saved is better than ten dead. Remember, the team assaults only as a last resort. What if four of the ten hostages are saved, but we lose five SWAT operators? This represents a higher loss rate than if the assault wasn't committed, a demonstrable failure.

The point is, *don't plan for acceptable losses.* If acceptable losses are mentioned, the plan is probably poor; re-evaluate for an acceptable loss rate of zero. This does not disregard SWAT's risk factor; that is part of the job. There is a great difference between possible losses and planned losses. Tactical success doesn't always equate with mission success. A normal life circumstance concerning the leader occurs when good intentions spawn unintended results. Remember, victories are readily shared, but few people ever claim their share in defeat. Plan for the worst, hope for the best.

Chapter 5
TACTICAL TIPS

The team leader must be extremely tactically proficient. The following is a list of helpful reminders. This list is not intended to be all-inclusive.

WEAPONS

A. The team leader must be familiar with and know all assigned weapons functioning, characteristics, and capabilities.

B. Cross-train all team members on all assigned weapons.

C. Dual-clipped or taped opposing magazines are prone to collecting dirt and debris in the inverted magazine.

D. Dropping the M16 series rifle on its butt may cause a round to chamber or fire.

E. High-capacity magazines may cause the operator to monopod in the prone position. This condition causes the firing platform to become unstable, causes malfunctions, and presents the adversary with a larger target.

F.   Before entering the tactical arena, ensure all weapons are hot by examining the chamber, checking dual-feed magazine round position, and press checking or observing loaded round indicator devices.

G.   Ensure that weapon lights are secure and operable.

H.   Select ammunition type and amount based on mission profile.

I.   Ensure rear sights are set accordingly and weapons are zeroed.

J.   Load the bottom three rounds in each magazine with tracers. This provides the operator with a visual indicator that he needs to reload.

K.   The leader should carry one magazine of straight tracers for field-expedient target identification. Remember that tracers work both ways. Shoot/move and communicate.

L.   Tape all sling swivels, but do not remove slings.

M.   Check all magazines to ensure they are clean and loaded properly.

N.   Check all weapons for cleanliness and functioning.

O.   Carry all magazines upside-down with the bullets toward the belt buckle. This keeps dirt and water out as well as facilitates loading.

P.   When loading magazines, inspect them for binding and cleanliness.

Q.   Don't ride the bolt forward on any semiauto.

LOAD-BEARING EQUIPMENT

A. Standardize equipment location.

B. Don't place anything on the right or left shoulder. Leave these weapon pockets clear since the operator may have to shoot from either side. (Just try to mount and fire the long gun when it's resting on a K-bar.)

C. Only carry what is necessary for the mission profile.

D. Always carry a flashlight, even on day operations.

E. Tape all snaps and buckles.

F. Always carry a knife.

G. Only straighten one leg on distraction device pins.

H. Don't hang distraction devices by their pins. Carry them in a Kevlar-backed leg pouch.

I. Ensure that distraction device fuses are tight.

J. Attach a spare distraction device pin to your gear. This is used to re-pin a device that has been armed and the pin discarded.

K. Use waterproof bags to protect equipment during inclement weather operations.

L. Adjust gear to fit over body armor.

M. Always carry maps and notebooks in waterproof containers.

N. Carry several pencils to make notes with. Ink smears

or runs dry; lead will not.

O. If you must cough, cough into a hat or cloth to smother the noise.

P. Always carry a spare flashlight and radio batteries.

Q. Don't wear unnecessary equipment.

R. Make sure tactical gloves are tight; loose gloves interfere with weapons manipulation.

SCHEME OF MANEUVER

A. Plan the route from the line of departure to the completion of the mission.

B. Identify phase lines and rally points.

C. Inspect all uniforms, equipment, and camouflage prior to departure.

D. Observe halt and listening points. Rest as applicable. Listen half the amount of time the team moves.

E. Stay alert at all times. Observe 360-degree security. When halting, drop to a minimum of one knee with weapon pointed outboard. Always check 40 to 60 meters all around.

F. If operating in rural areas, put insect repellent around tops of boots, on pants fly, belt area, and cuffs to stop insects.

G. Check the point man to make sure he is on course and for fatigue. Change out as necessary.

H. Avoid overconfidence; just because the team hasn't seen the suspect doesn't mean he hasn't seen the team.

I. Observe noise discipline.

J. Correct team or individual errors as they occur.

K. Each team member must continually observe the man in front and the man behind.

L. When crossing danger areas, observe and listen first, choose a sound tactical formation, then breach same.

M. Keep radio transmissions to a minimum in order to thwart monitoring.

N. Never set patterns during the scheme of maneuver.

O. Don't wear jewelry during the operation; it may give the team's position away through reflection and can snag on a variety of items.

P. Do not wear watches with hourly chimes, alarms, or that are brightly illuminated.

Q. Make eye contact with the operator targeted to receive a hand signal. If he doesn't see it, it won't be received.

R. Call suspects out of their positions; don't go after them.

S. Don't hound dog suspects (run after them), as this is usually a diversion or ambush; continue with the mission.

T. Clear stairs from the top down if possible. This is much easier and safer.

U. Travel through buildings (that aren't occupied) instead of around them. This provides cover, concealment, ease of movement, and speed.

V. Take advantage of dead space and ambient noise. If the team can't be seen, move rapidly. If the team can't be heard, consider moving rapidly if this is conducive to cover. However, don't throw caution to the wind.

W. Initiate the assault when the suspect is fatigued, inattentive, or diverted. A good traditional time frame is around 0400.

X. Unless total surprise is achieved, the suspect will normally be located in the corner of the room, have his back to the wall, be facing the door, be as near to the floor as possible, or be hiding behind an object.

Y. When moving, minimize fatigue; tired men become careless.

Z. When considering a tactical option, weigh the process with the intended outcome. For example, if the lights are on in a structure, does the power need to be shut off in order to diminish the suspect's vision? If so, the SWAT team will need to utilize night vision devices or flashlight techniques. Is the team proficient under these circumstances? If not, the leader may choose to leave the power on so the SWAT team and suspects are even. Each tactical option chosen should be expected to achieve an advantage for the SWAT team.

GENERAL TIPS

A. At a minimum, require the department's EOC representative to sign the operations order. The TOC commander's signature is a good idea as well.

B. If the team leader must leave the team prior to insertion, he informs the second in command where he is going and how long he will be gone. This ensures the team leader's expedient notification if the team gets the order to insert while he is absent.

C. Show confidence in the plan so the team will have confidence.

D. Seek advice and assistance from team members during planning.

E. Always keep an alternate plan in mind.

F. Use tact when reprimanding team personnel.

G. It is the EOC's right and responsibility to order the assault. However, be careful if they are pushing the assault in order to cut down on overtime, in response to public pressure, to prevent inconveniencing the public, or to avoid paying housing costs for evacuees. The key is to make sure the mission is commensurate with the team's capabilities.

H. Develop target folders. These include priority target intel such as ingress/egress points, utility control locations, observation points, avenues of escape/approach, and so on.

I. Practice planning and the writing of the warning/operations order through test exercises.

J. If the mission is compromised, consider the effect on surprise, speed, and violence of action. Mission abortion may be required.

EPILOGUE

Perhaps I have been preaching to the choir. If this is the case, great! You, as a leader or aspiring leader, have attempted to broaden your knowledge base. That's a strong leadership trait, and it's a never-ending process. When a leader thinks he knows it all, failure is just around the corner. Hopefully, the consequences of this failure will not be felt in the gravest extreme.

If much of this information is new to you, that's great too! Hopefully, you have grasped the importance of SWAT leadership traits and tactical planning. Of course, once you reflect upon leadership traits, command structure, position duties, team configuration, weapon choices/placement, team movement and control, the planning process, warning order preparation, EOC/TOC/FCP operations, intelligence gathering, mission considerations, operations order preparation, debriefing procedures, and tactical tips to remember, you may not want to be a leader. Be advised, any SWAT member at any time may be pressed into the leader's role through exigent circumstances. Now you have the knowledge to do something.

Finally, if nothing else has been gained, surely an appreciation for SWAT leadership duties has been realized. If you learned a trick or two, try implementing them in a future mission, then compare your team's performance to past missions. If just one concept in this whole book saves a SWAT officer's or innocent person's life, my goal will have been reached. Of course, we will all benefit if adversaries are more efficiently neutralized.

INDEX

A

Ammunition 17, 26, 55, 60, 71, 89, 92, 95, 104
Assault team(s) 19, 20, 78, 80, 91
Assault team leader(s) 73, 82
Assistant CNT leader(s) 83
Assistant team leader 17, 19, 20
Assistant TOC coordinator 78, 83

B

Base of fire 48, 52, 58, 60
Bounding overwatch 45, 48, 52, 55
Breach/breaching 63, 67, 100, 107

C

Chain of command 1, 20, 71, 73, 75, 77, 96, 97, 99
CNT leader 82
Column formation 34, 45
Compromise procedures 72, 75, 93, 94
Cover man 4, 14, 17, 19, 21, 67
Crisis negotiation team (CNT) 77, 78, 79

D

E

F

H

I

L

N

O

P

R

S